PRAYER

AND THE

VOICE OF GOD

Phillip D. Jensen
and Tony Payne

Guidebooks for Life 🯅

Bible-based essentials
for your Christian journey

Prayer and the Voice of God is part of a series of
straightforward, practical Christian books from
Matthias Media which deal with the important nuts-
and-bolts topics that Christians need to know about
as we walk each day with our Master.

Some Christian books are all theory and no practical
application; others are all stories and tips with
no substance. The Guidebooks for Life aim to
achieve a vital balance—that is, to dig into the Bible
and discover what God is telling us there, as well
as applying that truth to our daily Christian lives.

For up-to-date information about the latest
Guidebooks for Life, visit our website:
www.matthiasmedia.com.au

GUIDEBOOKS FOR LIFE

PRAYER

AND THE

VOICE OF GOD

LISTENING TO GOD'S LIVING WORD WILL
TRANSFORM THE WAY YOU PRAY

*Phillip D. Jensen
and Tony Payne*

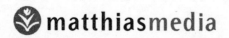

matthiasmedia

Prayer and the Voice of God
© Matthias Media 2006

Matthias Media
(St Matthias Press Ltd. ACN 067 558 365)
PO Box 225
Kingsford NSW 2032 Australia
Telephone: (02) 9663 1478; international: +61 2 9663 1478
Facsimile: (02) 9663 3265; international: +61 2 9663 3265
Email: info@matthiasmedia.com.au
Internet: www.matthiasmedia.com.au

ISBN 1 921068 28 0

Cover design and typesetting by Lankshear Design Pty Ltd.

CONTENTS

Chapter 1

PRAYER AND GOD'S VOICE

PRAYER IS JUST ABOUT THE MOST naturally unnatural thing it is possible to do.

It is natural because anyone can do it, and most people do it at one stage or other in their lives. Even the most hardened atheist will throw a hopeful prayer skywards in his darkest hour. We know a man who did just this when caught on board a ship in a typhoon. He promised that if God would rescue him from the storm, he would find out more about God and how to serve him. God did and he did.

Desperate atheists can do it, children can do it, little old ladies can do it. 'Prayer' is not hard. It seems almost to be a spontaneous activity that simply happens to nearly everyone from time to time. It's natural.

And yet it is also very unnatural, almost by definition. When people pray, they are seeking an intervention in the natural course of events. They want their 'god'—whatever they perceive him, her or it to be—to do something for them that otherwise would not have happened. They want super-nature to invade nature for their benefit: to heal sickness, to right an injustice, to perform a typhoon rescue.

It's unnatural in another sense, too, as anyone who has tried to pray for any length of time will tell you. The occasional desperate prayer in a time of need is not too taxing. But praying regularly, consistently and faithfully—that's another matter. Most Christians will testify to the **difficulty** of prayer. If the Bible is any guide, we have to be taught to pray, and then encouraged, exhorted and even commanded to continue doing it. When the Apostle Paul mentions that his good friend and colleague Epaphras has been 'wrestling' or 'struggling' in prayer (for the Colossians; see Col 4:12), we recognize the experience. Prayer often feels like a wrestling match—with God, with our circumstances, with our own weakness. Indeed, as we look more closely at prayer in this book, we will need to come to terms with not only why and how we should pray, but also why we **don't** pray, for prayerlessness is a common and besetting sin for many Christians.

Our first step, however, is more basic but no less important. Before we go any further, we need to take a moment to define what we mean by 'prayer', for there are a great many different activities in the world that are referred to as 'prayer'.

Prayer in some religious traditions is not so much asking the deity for something as simply reciting a set form of holy words (like the five-times-daily 'prayer' in Islam). In other cultures, prayer can be silent meditation, an exalted state of consciousness, the affixing of petitions to prayer wheels that spin in the wind, a wild whirling dance of religious ecstasy, the offering of gifts or the lighting of candles.

Christians, too, can mean different things when they talk about prayer. In Christian circles, any of the following practices might be labelled as 'prayer':

- silent adoration of God, or silent meditation on his character or word;
- an action performed with God in mind (as in the Keith Green song, 'Make my life a prayer to you');
- giving thanks to God;
- praising God in song;
- confessing our sins to God;
- making requests of God;
- waiting or listening for God's voice to come to us.

The final item on that list—seeking to listen for God's voice in prayer—is a subject that we will think about more as we proceed. At this point, however, we need to focus on God's voice in a different sense. If we are going to understand true prayer, and pray how God wants us to, then our first step must be to **listen to what God has to say about prayer**. For it is not what we think about prayer that matters, but what God thinks about prayer. We must allow God, who created prayer, to tell us what prayer is, to shape our thinking about prayer, to fire our hearts with the motivation to pray, and to teach us how and when and what we should pray. We must turn, in other words, to God's living word in the Bible and listen humbly to what he has to say to us about this vital subject.

This, of course, is hard for us to do—not because the Bible is very difficult to understand on this subject, nor because we lack the opportunity to listen to it, but because our natural sinful tendency is to ignore God's voice whenever possible. We would rather define prayer (or define God, for that matter) in a way that seems good to us—which suits us. We prefer to listen to the voice of our own reason, the voice of our friends or the voice of popular opinion, than to listen with trembling to the voice of God.

Yet this is what we must do if we are to pray in a way that honours the God who created prayer and who initiates our prayers by revealing himself to us and drawing us into relationship with himself.

When we do turn to listen to God's voice in the Bible, we discover a very interesting thing. People today may refer to any number of different activities as 'prayer' but when God speaks about 'prayer' in the Bible, he is really only talking about one thing. In the

Bible, 'prayer' simply means **"asking God for things"**.[1]

This may seem like a rather simplistic definition—a definition that just states the obvious—but, given how confused Christians can be about prayer, it's where we need to start. There are three important things to notice in this definition.

Firstly, 'prayer' in the Bible is **asking** for something. This is what the biblical words we translate as 'pray' or 'prayer' mean. In fact, many of these words are also used of asking humans for things as well—for example, the Greek word translated 'pray' in Acts 8:24 is the same word the Ethiopian eunuch uses just a few verses later when he 'asks' Phillip to explain the Bible to him (v. 34). To 'pray' is to present a request or supplication or petition to another person, and very often in the Bible that person is God.

Now there are lots of other verbal activities we engage in with people: we thank them, chat to them,

---

[1]   In the New Testament, for example, the most common Greek word for 'prayer' is *proseuche* (and its verbal form *proseuchomai*, 'to pray'). In its different forms, it occurs 121 times in the New Testament. On some occasions, it is used without the activity being described or defined (e.g. "Jesus went up on the mountain by himself to pray"). But whenever the activity is described or defined in some way, or the meaning of the word is made clear by its context, *proseuche* and *proseuchomai* always refer to the act of asking or requesting or seeking something from God. The other two Greek words that are sometimes translated 'to pray' are the everyday words *aitew* ('to ask, ask for, demand') and *deomai* ('to ask, request, beseech, beg').

inform them of things, joke with them or even tell them how good they are (that is, praise them). We also listen to what they have to say to us. But the word 'prayer' means to **ask** someone for something. It's the same with our talking to God. It is perfectly right—indeed obligatory—that we thank God for his many gifts to us, but strictly speaking we are not 'praying' when we do this, not in the way the Bible uses the word. It is also great to pause in the midst of our busyness and contemplate how good and wonderful God is, and to mull over in our minds his many perfections and merciful deeds—but this is not 'prayer'. It is also our privilege as Christians to praise God—that is, to tell each other and all the world, and even God himself, how glorious and mighty God is—how he has rescued us and showered us with one blessing after another. We can 'praise' God in song, in poetry, in spoken words or even in print. But this also is not 'prayer'—not in the way the Bible uses the word. Nor is prayer in the Bible 'listening to God'. It is vital that we pay careful and obedient attention to every word that proceeds from the mouth of God, but the activity of doing so is never called 'prayer' in the Bible.

It's very helpful to get this clear in our minds. Thanksgiving ought always to accompany 'prayer' but it is not itself 'prayer'. Meditating on God's word and character is a marvellous thing to do, and, indeed, it can prompt us to pray, but meditation is not 'prayer'. Prayer is asking God for something. If we are to avoid confusion as we seek to listen to what God has to say about prayer, we must make sure that we are speaking the same language as he does in the Scriptures. When God speaks about 'prayer', he is speaking about 'asking for something'.

Secondly, 'prayer' is about asking **a person**—in this case, God—to do something. As we've noted, the words for 'prayer' in the Bible also mean to ask human persons for things. But when they refer to asking God for something, we usually translate them as 'pray' in English. To pray is to address yourself to a 'somebody'— to a person. It's a relational activity. It is silly to 'pray' to a rock or a tree in the way the Bible uses the word 'pray', because rocks and trees cannot hear and respond. They can't be asked for things. But the God of the Bible, as we shall see, is a God that **can** be asked for things.

This brings us to the third and final point worth noticing in our little definition, which is that prayer always involves **words**. Asking a person for something involves speaking to them—making a verbal request. That is why 'prayer' in the Bible is not silent contemplation or the babbling repetition of meaningless phrases or the flying of flags or the spinning of wheels. Prayer in the Bible is unashamedly and universally verbal.

So prayer is 'asking God for something'. This very simple biblical definition of prayer may raise all sorts of questions in our minds. What is the place of thanksgiving? What about confession? What about meditation?

We will return to these questions in due course.

Firstly, however, we need to continue what we have only just begun: listening to God's voice and learning from him the foundations of prayer.

Chapter 2

THE GOD OF PRAYER

AT THE FRONT OF THE ROOM there is a well-fed, prosperous-looking man at ease in his surroundings. He stands with the confidence of an insider, not the embarrassed solitude of a newcomer. He holds his head back, his face turned up to heaven: "God, I thank you that I am not like other men, extortioners, unjust, adulterers, or even like this tax collector. I fast twice a week; I give tithes of all that I get." He is so pleased with himself and his righteousness that he doesn't get around to 'praying' at all. He has no need to ask God for anything; he is already the best of men.

At the rear, a very different man hunches not far from the door, standing in one spot, his only movement the steady arc of his fist, which he repeatedly hammers against his own chest. His face is turned down, as if by looking up he might catch the eye of someone who will ask him to leave. His prayer is faltering and simple: "God, be merciful to me, a sinner!"

Two different men; two very different prayers.

The Bible often has strong contrasts in prayer like this one (from Luke 18). Picture, for example, the babbling pagans of Matthew 6 who heap phrase upon phrase, thinking that the more words they send in God's direction, the more likely they are to be heard. Compare their prattling to the simple 52-word prayer which Jesus teaches his disciples in the same chapter.

Perhaps the greatest contrast of all is found in Elijah's prayer contest with the prophets of Baal in 1 Kings 18. This momentous battle took place at a time in Israel's history when the people were faced with a stark choice. The prophet Elijah laid it before them very simply: "How long will you go limping between two different opinions? If the LORD[1] is God, follow him; but if Baal, then follow him" (v. 21). To help them make up their minds, Elijah issues a challenge to the prophets of Baal who are assembled there with all the Israelites on Mt Carmel. "It's a simple test", says Elijah. "We'll both

---

[1]   Where the word 'LORD' or 'GOD' appears in small capitals in the Bible text, it stands for the four-letter Hebrew name for God, YHWH, which is pronounced something like 'Yahweh'. This is the holy name of God which he revealed to Moses at the burning bush in Exodus 3.

put a bull on an altar and we'll pray to our respective gods, and the one who answers by sending fire to burn up the sacrifice will be the true God"(if you'll pardon the paraphrase).

"Sounds fair enough", the people say, and the contest begins. As it unfolds, the two sides could not be more different. The prophets of Baal—all 450 of them—pray loud and long from morning till noon, calling upon Baal to answer them. They cut themselves with swords and lances, and continue to 'rave on', as the Bible text puts it, until late afternoon. But the heavens are stonily silent. There is no answer and no fire.

Elijah steps forward, just one man against 450. He pours water all over the sacrifice—not once but three times—just to make it more difficult and to ensure that no-one mentions the possibility of spontaneous combustion. And then he calls upon his God—not repeatedly for six hours but just once, with a simple prayer lasting no more than 30 seconds:

> "O Lord, God of Abraham, Isaac, and Israel, let it
> be known this day that you are God in Israel, and
> that I am your servant, and that I have done all
> these things at your word. Answer me, O Lord,
> answer me, that this people may know that you,
> O Lord, are God, and that you have turned their
> hearts back." (1 Kings 18:36b-37)

Elijah's God answers immediately with blistering fire, burning up not only the bull, but the water-soaked wood, stones and dust, and licking up the water that had spilled down into the trench around the altar.

The prayer contest turns out to be no contest at all. And the fundamental difference between Elijah and the prophets of Baal is the two 'gods' they prayed to. One can hear and respond; the other cannot. One can act with power in the world; the other can do nothing. One is real; the other is not.

Prayer is determined to a very large extent by the kind of god you pray to. If your 'god' is an impersonal, mystical force rather than a person, then prayer will consist of aligning yourself with that force in some way—tuning into it, and learning to manipulate and use it. If your god is a nature god with a bad temper, you will constantly be trying to appease him by sacrifices and offerings, or by cutting yourself with swords and lances. If your god is a fertility god, you might persuade him to increase the harvest by performing sexual rituals in his temple.

The God of the Bible is none of these. At the most basic level, because he is a personal God, prayer to him consists of words—of asking him for things. But that is only the beginning. To understand Christian prayer, we need to do some more thinking about the God to whom we pray.

The source for that thinking will be the Bible, where God's voice is heard. In the Bible, God speaks to us and reveals to us what he is like, what he has done and what his plans are. Of course we could fill this whole book, and many more besides, discussing what the Scriptures tell us about God. Indeed, there is no better way to energize our prayer lives than to read the Scriptures, and know God better through them. In this chapter, we will look at five important aspects of God that are the foundation of Christian prayer.

1. The able God

The first and most basic teaching of the Bible about God is that he created the world from scratch—that he is not resident in some part of the creation, or suffused throughout the creation, but is outside it and beyond it. He is to the world as a potter is to his clay, forming and shaping it as he wishes, retaining complete power over it. God rules the world. It is his and he is God over it.

This aspect of God is written all over the Bible. In Psalm 33, to take just one example, we read this majestic description of a God who made all and who sits enthroned over all:

> By the word of the LORD the heavens were made,
>   and by the breath of his mouth all their host.
> He gathers the waters of the sea as a heap;
>   he puts the deeps in storehouses.
> Let all the earth fear the LORD;
>   let all the inhabitants of the world stand in awe of him!

For he spoke, and it came to be;
  he commanded, and it stood firm ...
The LORD looks down from heaven;
  he sees all the children of man;
from where he sits enthroned he looks out
  on all the inhabitants of the earth,
he who fashions the hearts of them all
  and observes all their deeds. (vv. 6-9, 13-15)

This is the God to whom we pray. He's not the non-entity conjured up in the imagination of the prophets of Baal. He's not an uninvolved or uninterested being who is no longer connected with his creation. And most certainly he is not a weak or powerless creature who is able to do some things but not others. He is the mighty creator and ruler of the world who can do anything. Jeremiah begins one of his prayers by crying out, "Ah, Lord GOD! It is you who has made the heavens and the earth by your great power and by your outstretched arm! Nothing is too hard for you" (Jer 32:17). And Jesus, at the time of his greatest anguish in Gethsemane, begins his prayer in the same way: "Abba, Father, all things are possible for you. Remove this cup from me. Yet not what I will, but what you will" (Mark 14:36).

In other words, we pray to a God who is supremely **able**, whose powers are so great that no action within the world is beyond him, no matter how small or detailed or large or extraordinary. Nothing is impossible for him.

2. The fatherly God

The Bible also makes it very clear that God not only created the world but continues to care for it and sustain it. Creation is not a self-powering, closed system that churns on without any involvement from its manufacturer; it is the creation of a loving God who continues to provide for, sustain and nourish it, as a father does for his children.

Paul strikes this note as he talks to the Athenians about the God that they need to get to know:

> "The God who made the world and everything in it, being Lord of heaven and earth, does not live in temples made by man, nor is he served by human hands, as though he needed anything, since he himself gives to all mankind life and breath and everything ... Yet he is actually not far from each one of us, for 'In him we live and move and have our being'; as even some of your own poets have said, 'For we are indeed his offspring'." (Acts 17:24-25, 27-28)

In a general sense, all of us are God's offspring. He created us, and he gives us life and breath and everything. And God is a generous father to all he has made, making his sun to shine on both the evil and the good, and sending rain on the just and unjust alike (Matt 5:45). He is a caring, loving God, whose mighty power is matched by his unfailing love for his creatures.

In other words, God is not only able, he is also very **willing** to care for his creation and grant good things to all his creatures. See how the psalmist describes God's constant detailed concern for the whole created order:

> From your lofty abode you water the mountains;
> the earth is satisfied with the fruit of your work.
> You cause the grass to grow for the livestock
> and plants for man to cultivate,
> that he may bring forth food from the earth
> and wine to gladden the heart of man,
> oil to make his face shine
> and bread to strengthen man's heart ...
> The young lions roar for their prey,
> seeking their food from God.
> When the sun rises, they steal away
> and lie down in their dens.
> Man goes out to his work
> and to his labour until the evening.
> O LORD, how manifold are your works!
> In wisdom have you made them all;
> the earth is full of your creatures ...
> These all look to you,
> to give them their food in due season.
> When you give it to them, they gather it up;
> when you open your hand, they are filled with
> good things. (Ps 104:13-15, 21-24, 27-28)

So the God we pray to is powerful and supremely able, and in his fatherly care of us, he is very willing to give us good things. But there is more to say, for all this would be of little benefit to us if we couldn't communicate with God—that is, if we weren't able to speak to him, and he wasn't able and willing to listen to us.

3. The speaking and listening God

The Bible writers are not shy about blowing raspberries from time to time, and nothing invites their derision more often than the false gods and idols of the nations. Notice the sarcasm in the following passage from Psalm 115, where the psalmist contrasts the living, all-powerful God of Israel with the dead, powerless idols of the surrounding nations:

> Why should the nations say,
>   "Where is their God?"
> Our God is in the heavens;
>   he does all that he pleases.
> Their idols are silver and gold,
>   the work of human hands.
> They have mouths, but do not speak;
>   eyes, but do not see.
> They have ears, but do not hear;
>   noses, but do not smell.
> They have hands, but do not feel;
>   feet, but do not walk;
>   and they do not make a sound in their throat.
> (Ps 115:2-7)

Asking an idol for something is utterly pointless—not only because the idol does not have any power or ability to grant the request, but because the idol can't hear you. It's a lump of silver or gold. That's all it is.

Around 30% of people in Western societies express some confidence in astrology, believing that the stars influence or determine our characters and the events of our lives. But you cannot pray to the stars. Or rather, you can if you wish, but you're wasting your time. The stars are inanimate and impersonal. They cannot hear or see or smell. They do not know or remember or respond or bless. They have as much power to listen to your prayers as the paperweight on your desk.

However, the real God who made heaven and earth is alive and active and personal and relational. He speaks and listens; he acts and helps; he remembers and blesses. He has both a voice and an ear.

Christian prayer relies on the fact that God has a voice. He speaks to us and reveals himself to us. He tells us of his plans and character. And he makes great and precious promises that we can trust and call upon him to fulfil.

However, prayer is also dependent upon God having an ear, if we can put it like that. God has created us with the ability to speak to him and ask for him for things (which is what prayer is), and he in turn is able to listen to our words. It is no accident that we have the capacity to speak to God with words, and that he has the capacity to hear and understand us. Words are part of the very nature of God and the creatures he has made. "In the beginning was the Word, and the Word was with God, and the Word was God" (John 1:1). God is the original wordsmith. And when he created humanity, he created us as persons who speak. To express our minds through speech is a vital part of what makes us human.

In contrast, it's interesting to note that praying to idols is **de**-humanizing. The psalm we quoted above continues, "Those who make them become like them; so do all who trust in them" (Ps 115:8). The dumb, inhuman, inanimate idols reduce their worshippers to the same state. We see this in the prayer practices of so many other religions whose adherents sit for hours wordlessly with an empty mind, rock from side to side while repeating mantras, whirl like dervishes, slash their bodies like Baal worshippers, or engage in human sacrifice like the Moabites or the Aztecs. In seeking to relate to that which is not God, they become that which is not human.

By contrast, praying to the real God—the personal, speaking, listening God—makes us fully human. We speak to him as persons, and he hears and listens to us as our personal creator.

If this is what the God we pray to is like, we can see more clearly why Christian prayer can be very simply defined as 'asking God for things'. For if the God we pray to is a powerful creator and generous fatherly provider, and if he is a speaking and listening God who makes creatures in his image who can communicate with him, then our prayers will take the form of speech, and we will look to our creator and ask him to act in his world.

However, there is another facet of God's character that we also must consider in relation to prayer. It is one that, far from encouraging us to pray, makes prayer seem impossible.

4. The holy God

So far we've emphasized our **similarity** to God as one of the foundations of prayer. Because God is personal and because he has created us to be persons as well, we can relate to God and he to us. Speaking and listening can take place on both sides.

But there is an equally important sense in which God is so different from us—so distinct and separate and 'other' from us—that we might wonder how 'asking him for things' might ever be possible. We are speaking of what the Bible calls God's 'holiness'—his separateness and distinctness from us, not only in might and power and wisdom and glory, but also in goodness and purity. The problem that God's holiness poses for prayer is simple: if, as Habakkuk puts it, God is too pure to look on evil, and cannot tolerate wrong (Hab 1:13), and if, as Paul says, all of humanity is under sin, with no-one righteous, not even one (Rom 3:9-10), how then can we ever hope to get a hearing before God? God may be able and willing to listen to us, but if the doors of his throne room are shut tight against us, how can our requests ever come before him? What makes us think that we will ever be good enough or pure enough to get past the door, let alone penetrate the blinding unapproachable light of his presence (1 Tim 6:16)?

The holiness of God was vividly represented to the people of Israel in the tabernacle (or 'tent') where God dwelt, and in the elaborate system of sacrifices and offerings that were required before any approach could be made to God's presence. The physical arrangement of the tabernacle said it all: the further you went in, the more impenetrable the barriers to God's presence became. At the very centre, in a small curtained-off space, there was the Most Holy Place, in which sat the ark of the covenant. This was where God's presence dwelt. Into this place only the High Priest could go, just once a year and only after elaborate rituals and blood-sacrifices were carried out to cleanse himself. The whole arrangement screamed out: "Danger! You can't come in here."

Many Christians don't think of God like this—as someone who "dwells in unapproachable light", "a consuming fire" or someone who pours out "wrath and fury" on the unrighteous. They might acknowledge that the God of the Old Testament was a bit like this on one of his bad days, but not the Christian God, the God of love and niceness. But all the above descriptions in quotation marks come from the New Testament (see 1 Tim 6:16, Heb 12:29 and Rom 2:8 respectively). The God of Jesus is a holy and pure God, who casts the unrighteous into hell (e.g. Luke 12:5; Matt 23:33).

God was and is and always will be a holy God, and this, when combined with our sinfulness, represents a seemingly impassable barrier to prayer. As Isaiah puts it:

> Behold, the LORD's hand is not shortened, that it
> cannot save,
>   or his ear dull, that it cannot hear;

but your iniquities have made a separation
    · between you and your God,
and your sins have hidden his face from you
    so that he does not hear. (Isa 59:1-2)

And this brings us to the fifth and final thing about the
God we pray to.

5. The merciful God

The truth can become so familiar that it ceases to
shock us or produce any reaction in us at all. Yet this
truth—which is the throbbing heartbeat of the whole
Bible—should never cease to arouse wonder and fear
and heartbreak and joy in us all at once.

This truth is that **God is merciful**. We see it in the
old covenant where, despite his blinding holiness and
Israel's stubborn sinfulness, God graciously and
constantly rescues his people, dwells in their midst,
listens to their prayers, and provides a means for them
to approach him and find forgiveness (the sacrificial
system). The psalmist says:

O you who hears prayer,
    to you shall all flesh come.
When iniquities prevail against me,
    you atone for our transgressions.
Blessed is the one you choose and bring near,
    to dwell in your courts!
We shall be satisfied with the goodness of your house,
    the holiness of your temple! (Ps 65:2-4)

What the merciful God did initially and partially under the old covenant, he did finally and completely under the new. He came himself to completely destroy the barrier between man and God, not by compromising his holiness or setting it aside, but by dealing once and for all with our uncleanness. At a particular time and place in human history, God the Father sent his own son into the world to bear the sins of the world in his body on the cross. Of the many places in the New Testament where Jesus' sacrificial death is explained, the book of Hebrews offers one of the most striking descriptions. "Remember how only the High Priest could enter the Most Holy Place? And only once a year and with blood?" says the author (our paraphrase). "Well, what Jesus has done on the cross makes it possible for us to enter an even Holier Place than that—heaven itself." He puts it like this:

> But when Christ appeared as a high priest of
> the good things that have come, then through the
> greater and more perfect tent (not made with
> hands, that is, not of this creation) he entered once
> for all into the holy places, not by means of the
> blood of goats and calves but by means of his own
> blood, thus securing an eternal redemption. For
> if the sprinkling of defiled persons with the blood
> of goats and bulls and with the ashes of a heifer
> sanctifies for the purification of the flesh, how
> much more will the blood of Christ, who through
> the eternal Spirit offered himself without blemish
> to God, purify our conscience from dead works to
> serve the living God. (Heb 9:11-14)

The consequence of Jesus' redeeming death is that there is no longer any barrier between God and us. Now—incredibly, wondrously—we can **draw near** to the holy God, clothed in the bright, clean robes of Christ, and speak to the Father and present our requests before him. The writer of Hebrews continues:

> Therefore, brothers, since we have confidence to enter the holy places by the blood of Jesus, by the new and living way that he opened for us through the curtain, that is, through his flesh, and since we have a great priest over the house of God, let us draw near with a true heart in full assurance of faith, with our hearts sprinkled clean from an evil conscience and our bodies washed with pure water. (Heb 10:19-22)

This offer of mercy—of cleansing, of intimate relationship with the holy God of the universe—is open to all. It's the word of the gospel, the proclamation of the incredible news that Jesus has come and died and risen as the Lord and saviour of the world. Here again we see how prayer depends upon God's initiative and his voice. Prayer is only possible because God calls and summons us by the gospel to enter a relationship with himself.

Our response to the message of the gospel is to accept and act upon it—to turn our backs on our old, rebellious way of life and put our trust in the Lord Jesus Christ. In the Bible's words, we do this by **repentance** and **faith**.

'Repentance' is a simple idea. It means 'a turn-around'. To repent is to make a fundamental change in mindset and direction. To 'repent' towards God means to stop going the way we were going (that is, our own selfish way), to turn around and to head back in the right direction. It means committing ourselves to living God's way, obeying him, serving him and pleasing him.

'Faith' is also not very complex, although it is often misunderstood. To have faith in someone is simply to trust them or rely upon them. To trust or to have faith in Jesus is to rely on his sacrificial death as the only way our sins can be forgiven.

It's like being caught in a rip-tide and dragged out to sea. You're floundering there, the swell is choppy and the beach is gradually receding into the distance. You realize that you will never be able to swim back to shore and you are almost certainly going to drown. The situation appears hopeless. At that moment, a man on a surfboard paddles up alongside you and says, "I can save you. Grab hold of my board and I'll tow you back to the beach."

Now, faith is not saying to yourself, "Oh look, there's a man with a surfboard", nor is it saying to yourself, "I guess if I grab his board I'll have a reasonable chance of being saved". Faith or trust in this circumstance is grabbing hold of the board with all your strength, and hanging on tight all the way back to shore.

Faith in Jesus is 'grabbing hold' of his death as the only way out of the desperate plight we are in with

God. It's putting all our trust in him—trusting that he will save us from God's rightful anger at our sin.

There's something else about repentance and faith that requires us to change our life-saving illustration a little. It is not just that we are in a predicament or that we can't save ourselves; we're not simply the unfortunate victims of an unfavourable tide. The depressing truth is that we are deliberately swimming away from the shore—away from safety—and that we are the lifesaver's enemies. We do not want to be rescued and we will not even admit that we are in danger, even as we swallow mouthfuls of water and cast frightened glances over our shoulder at the faraway beach. In truth, the lifesaver has to take matters into his own hands—pluck us out of the water, wrap our tired arms around his board, and keep one hand upon us to make sure we hang on as he paddles back to shore. We are saved by the strength of his hold on us, not by the power of our hold on him.

God not only offers up his own Son to pay the penalty for our sins, but this Son, risen and ascended to glory, pours out his Spirit to bring new life to sinful rebels who want nothing to do with him. In other words, even our repentance and faith are gifts of God by his Spirit (Acts 11:18; 13:48). It is only through his own work in us that we are born anew and we rise to new spiritual life. It is only by the powerful action of his Spirit that our eyes are opened—that we look up and see the smiling face of the lifesaver and, with unspeakable gratitude, fling our arms around him.

THE GOD WE PRAY TO—the God revealed in the Scriptures —is the fatherly God, who created the world, and rules and cares for it still in all his power. And through the gospel of Christ, this fatherly God becomes **our** Father. Like estranged, rebellious children who have turned around and come home, we can now become members of his own family with the privilege of access into his presence.

This is the God we pray to. This gives our definition of Christian prayer a little more punch. Prayer is a work of God's Spirit within us such that we approach our heavenly Father in faith, through the merits and death of our Lord Jesus, to ask him for things. It's our relationship of dependence upon God expressed in words. Prayer is audible faith.

THE GOD OF PRAYER

Chapter 3

WHY PRAY?

We started in chapter 1 by saying that prayer is simply 'asking someone for something'. That's what the word means. But as we looked at 'the God of prayer' in chapter 2, we began to see that, in the end, prayer is not defined by a dictionary so much as by God himself. He is the fatherly creator of all the world who is both able and willing to provide all good things for his creatures. And we can ask him for things because he is the kind of God you can talk to, and because he has created us to be the kind of creatures who can speak. What's more, through the gospel of Jesus, God becomes **our** Father, who forgives our rebellion and sin, and graciously allows us into his holy presence to make our requests of him.

This is the first and most basic reason for prayer. We pray **because we can**—because God **allows us to**.

Let's think about this a little more, along with three other powerful reasons and motivations for prayer.

1. We pray because God allows us to

You park your car out the front of a large residence at 1600 Pennsylvania Ave, Washington D.C. There are armed guards on the gate but you walk straight past them without pausing. You then stroll towards the front door, nodding and smiling at the staff at all the security check points you pass on the way. In the entrance foyer, you are greeted personally and ushered through more security barriers into the interior of the house. Secret Service agents in black suits open doors for you as you wander down the various corridors, until you finally arrive at the room you're looking for. You open the door and walk into an oval-shaped office. You smile at the man sitting behind the large desk and say, "Morning, Dad. I was just passing by and was wondering whether you could do me a favour."

Imagine having that sort of access to the President of the United States of America. Imagine being able to pop in whenever it suited you to see the most powerful man in the world—to chat to him as a child to a father and know that he will not just be available to see you, but be happy to listen to anything you say and willing to help you out in any way he can.

God is the king of kings and the president of

presidents. He is the supreme creator and ruler of the whole world. He made the President of the United States from dust. The White House is like a piece on his Monopoly board. His security detail is made up of angels with flaming swords.

And yet this mighty, all-powerful God, who by rights should destroy us as his enemies, has instead reached out to us in love, wiped away our sins and adopted us as his own children. He has become our Father, and he allows us to approach him and pour out our requests to him at any time, promising that he will hear us and give us every good gift.

This is the first, and in a sense the only, necessary reason for prayer. We pray because of the extraordinary fact that we can—that God allows us to.

But it's more than simply being allowed to pray. Our relationship with God demands that we pray.

2. We pray because we must

From the very beginning of our Christian lives, prayer is not optional; it is necessary. For there can be no access to God, and no father-child relationship with God, unless our sins are dealt with through the death of Jesus. And we grasp hold of that death and make it our own by turning around from our rebellion, confessing our sin, begging God's forgiveness, and putting our whole trust in the power and effectiveness of Jesus' death to pay the price. The Christian life, in other words, starts with the tax collector's prayer: "O God, be merciful to me, a sinner!"

This is not only how the Christian life starts but also how it proceeds. We never stop being repentant sinners. If we pretend otherwise, we're kidding ourselves, as the Apostle John reminds us:

> But if we walk in the light, as he is in the light, we have fellowship with one another, and the blood of Jesus his Son cleanses us from all sin. If we say we have no sin, we deceive ourselves, and the truth is not in us. If we confess our sins, he is faithful and just to forgive us our sins and to cleanse us from all unrighteousness. If we say we have not sinned, we make him a liar, and his word is not in us.
>
> My little children, I am writing these things to you so that you may not sin. But if anyone does sin, we have an advocate with the Father, Jesus Christ the righteous. He is the propitiation for our sins, and not for ours only but also for the sins of the whole world. (1 John 1:7-2:2)

It's not that sinning is good or desirable. We should stop! But given that all of us do continue to do the wrong thing, the prayer of confession will always be our daily prayer, as will our urgent requests for God to lead us not into temptation, to deliver us from evil, and to give us the good gift of his Spirit so that we might walk in his ways.

Our relationship with God also demands constant

prayer because of the kind of relationship it is. We are dependent, trusting children; he is the loving, generous Father. How can such a relationship be real if the children never speak to their father, and express their dependence and trust in him by asking for his help? We are no longer rebels who snatch the Father's gifts but refuse to honour or thank him. We are no longer pagans who run after food and drink and clothes, as if our lives were entirely in our own hands, or as if these things were all that mattered in life. We are now the grateful recipients of his incredible grace and forgiveness who have come crawling back to him in repentance, and we now look to him to provide us with all that we need. We want to give him honour and glory in all that we do, and God is never more honoured and glorified than when we humbly ask him for things, when he grants them in his mighty power and generosity, and when we pour out our thanks to him for his kindness.

How could we have this sort of relationship with our heavenly Father without constantly coming before him to ask for his generous provision? It would be bizarre, perverse and wrong.

But there's the problem.

3. We pray because we are commanded to

Not praying may well be bizarre, perverse and wrong, but our problem is that we are still very capable of being bizarre, perverse and wrong. We continue to be sinful fools. We find ourselves lapsing back into the self-centred, self-sufficient mindset of our neighbours who think they don't need God, and who neither ask him for anything, nor thank him for the many blessings he showers upon them anyway. We forget God. We do precisely what Moses warned Israel **not** to do when they were about to enter the prosperous land God was giving them:

> "Take care lest you forget the LORD your God by not keeping his commandments and his rules and his statutes, which I command you today, lest, when you have eaten and are full and have built good houses and live in them, and when your herds and flocks multiply and your silver and gold is multiplied and all that you have is multiplied, then your heart be lifted up, and you forget the LORD your God, who brought you out of the land of Egypt, out of the house of slavery, who led you through the great and terrifying wilderness, with its fiery serpents and scorpions and thirsty ground where there was no water, who brought you water out of the flinty rock, who fed you in the wilderness with manna that your fathers did not know, that he might humble you and test you, to do you good in the end. Beware lest you say in your heart, 'My

power and the might of my hand have gotten me this wealth'." (Deut 8:11-17)

God, in his kindness, helps us even in our folly of neglecting prayer. He commands us to pray. He reminds and urges and exhorts us to pray. He calls out to us from the words of Scripture: "Don't forget to pray. Make sure you pray. Keep on praying." Here are just some of his commands:

> ... take the helmet of salvation, and the sword of the Spirit, which is the word of God, **praying at all times in the Spirit**, with all prayer and supplication. To that end keep alert with all perseverance, making supplication for all the saints ... (Eph 6:17-18)

> Rejoice always, **pray without ceasing**, give thanks in all circumstances; for this is the will of God in Christ Jesus for you. (1 Thess 5:16-18)

> Rejoice in hope, be patient in tribulation, **be constant in prayer**. (Rom 12:12)

> **Continue steadfastly in prayer**, being watchful in it with thanksgiving. (Col 4:2)

> "... **call upon me** in the day of trouble; I will deliver you, and you shall glorify me." (Ps 50:15)

He gives us these reminders and commands to pray like a father instructing his children, urging and directing them to do what is really in their best interests, but which they are slow and reluctant to do.

If you require a simple reason to pray, here it is: the God and ruler of the universe tells you to.

The flipside of this motivation for prayer is obvious, but it's worth reflecting on: if God commands us to pray constantly, then not to pray constantly is disobedience and sin. We shouldn't regard prayer as an optional extra to the Christian life, like a physical exercise plan that, predictably, falls into disuse and about which we shrug our shoulders and say, "Look I know I should, but life is just too busy. I'll get back to it one of these days." Prayerlessness is sinful. As Samuel says to the people of Israel:

> "Moreover, as for me, far be it from me that I
> should sin against the LORD by ceasing to pray for
> you ..." (1 Sam 12:23)

All Christians will fall into this sin at different times in their lives and, as with our other failings and mistakes, we must hear God's call, repent, seek his forgiveness and start again. Perhaps right here and now you need to make a fresh start with God.

4. We pray because of God's promise

Our final answer to the question, "Why pray?" rests upon another aspect of our relationship with God. It's in the verse from Psalm 50 that we quoted above:

"... call upon me in the day of trouble;
I will deliver you, and you shall glorify me." (Ps 50:15)

We pray because God has spoken and promised to hear our prayers and answer them. This is a powerful motivation. Not only does God grant us access to his throne through the blood of Jesus, but he promises that he will listen to us and grant us every good thing. Would we expect our loving, fatherly creator to do otherwise? As Jesus said:

> "Ask, and it will be given to you; seek, and you will find; knock, and it will be opened to you. For everyone who asks receives, and the one who seeks finds, and to the one who knocks it will be opened. Or which one of you, if his son asks him for bread, will give him a stone? Or if he asks for a fish, will give him a serpent? If you then, who are evil, know how to give good gifts to your children, how much more will your Father who is in heaven give good things to those who ask him!" (Matt 7:7-11)

We can trust our heavenly Father to give us good things in response to our prayers, and, as we trust his word and pray to him, we bring glory to him. Every time we open our mouths in prayer, we are saying, "I know you are able, I know you are willing, I know you are my creator and Father through the Lord Jesus Christ, and I know that you have promised to hear me when I call to you in prayer".

WE'VE LOOKED AT FOUR excellent reasons for prayer. We pray:

- because God allows us to;
- because our relationship with him demands it;
- because he commands us to;
- and because he so graciously promises to hear us.

Prayer is so obvious, so necessary, so right, so good, and so fruitful. The real question is, why on earth would we **not** pray?

Chapter 4

WHY WE DON'T PRAY

Iт was 6:52 ам. Roger checked to make sure he had everything. It was all there: the bonded-leather, cross-referenced, words-of-Christ-in-green NIV Eco-Bible; the notepad with personal prayer points arranged by day and subject; his church prayer diary; his missionary prayer diary; his worldwide student ministry prayer diary; his lectionary edition of *Anglicans: This Could Be Your Prayer Book*; and, in case all else failed, his dog-eared copy of the *Jesus Person Pocketbook of Life-changing Bible Promises*.

It was 6:57 am and, having made sure he had what he needed, Roger closed his eyes and tried to get in the mood. "Just focus on the majesty and goodness of God", he told himself. "The majesty and goodness of God ..."

At 7:00 am, Roger's digital watch beeped the hour. With a half-frown of annoyance, Roger thought to himself, "I really must figure out how to turn off that thing. Come to think of it, I'm not sure that I ever turned it on. Oh no. I hope it's not one of those watches where you get a beep on the hour whether you want it or not. I wouldn't be surprised, given how little I paid for it. Still, that's what Dad always used to say: 'You get what you pay for ...' Anyway, stop thinking about that. Back to prayer ... The majesty and goodness of God ..."

It was 7:04 am and Roger's mind drifted back to his watch. "Typical really. You lash this thing to your wrist as a so-called convenience, but what ends up happening? It interrupts everything. You can't even have a few minutes of quiet prayer without technology sticking its nose in. Maybe I should go watch-less for a while. Just live by the natural rhythms of life, like when we're on holidays ... Holidays ... We could really use a holiday. I wouldn't mind taking the kids to somewhere different this time— somewhere that would be a bit of a memory for them. But how could we afford to do that? Anyway, anyway, prayer! OK ... majesty and goodness ... Why don't I try the Lord's Prayer and see if that gets things started."

It was 7:10 am and Roger was just up to "deliver us from evil" when his four-year-old rushed into the bedroom and came and stood beside him with a solemn look on her face. "Matthew's got the peanut butter and he's wiping it all over the bed", she said. "Can I have breakfast now?"

For the first time that morning, Roger actually prayed: "Dear God, give me strength. And would you mind if we tried this again tomorrow morning?"

WHY IS IT LIKE THIS? What is it about prayer that, at the same time, both attracts and repels us? Why is it sometimes so easy, so encouraging and so comforting to call on our heavenly Father, and yet, at other times, so hard and dispiriting, as if we are talking to ourselves or, worse, to the ceiling?

A simple answer as to why we find prayer difficult might be, "Because we are sinful, hard-hearted fools". And that would be true enough. However, it's not a detailed-enough answer to help us. It would be like going to the doctor, telling him our symptoms and receiving the reply, "Your problem is that you're sick, and that's because humans are the kind of animals that get sick". True— even profound—but not very helpful as far as treatment is concerned. A more specific diagnosis is needed.

That's what we'll try to do in this chapter. We'll look in more detail at exactly why it is that sinful, hard-hearted fools like us fail to pray, despite the many excellent reasons and motivations for prayer that exist.

1. False views of God
As we've already seen, Christian prayer is based on the character of the true and living God, revealed in the

Bible. The God we pray to—the able, willing, listening, holy, saving God—is the one who really determines what Christian prayer is.

One of the main reasons we don't pray is that we absorb false, distorted views of God. We harbour misunderstandings about him, sometimes without even realizing that we're doing so. Sometimes these misunderstandings are relics of our non-Christian past —ideas that we picked up about God from our upbringing, from TV shows and movies, or from the views of our friends or schoolteachers or workmates. Sometimes they are the result of inaccurate or imbalanced teaching about God that we've absorbed as Christians.

Whatever their source, these false views of God are like undiagnosed spiritual tumours that sap the strength from our prayer lives.

a. We doubt whether God is able

One of the most common prayer-killing views of God is that he is not really able to act in his world in answer to our prayers. This misunderstanding comes in two forms.

The first is that God is limited by the natural laws that he has put in place to govern our world, and that he will not—in fact, **cannot**—intervene to change them. He can and does change us, so this view goes, and he helps us to deal with the harsh difficulties of life, but he doesn't intervene to redirect the course of nature itself.

This would seem to be a strange view to hold in

light of the Bible's repeated testimony to God acting dramatically in his world to alter the normal, 'natural' course of events. But it is a surprisingly widespread view, held by some influential Christian teachers—among them William Barclay. He writes:

> There is still another law of prayer which we must remember. Prayer moves within the natural laws which govern life. When we think of it, this is a necessity. The characteristic of this world is that it is a dependable world. If the laws that govern it were erratically suspended it would cease to become an order; it would become a chaos. Suppose a man was to accidentally fall from the 40th floor window of a New York skyscraper. Suppose him to be a good and devout man and a firm believer in prayer. Suppose him as he passes the 20th floor in his descent to pray, "O God, stop me falling". That is a prayer which cannot be answered, because at that moment that man is in the grip of the law of gravity, and to suspend that law of gravity would be to put an end, not to his fall, but the world in general.
>
> A very important conclusion follows from this. Prayer does not normally promise to achieve release from some situation; it brings power and endurance to meet and overcome that situation.[1]

---

[1] W. Barclay, *The Plain Man's Book of Prayers*, Fontana, London, 1959, p. 15.

One can only imagine the prayer that the man plummeting to his death might pray in order to "meet and overcome" his situation: "Dear Lord, I pray that, in this most difficult circumstance, you would grant me endurance so that I may—" SPLAT!

Mr Barclay's view of prayer is not only ridiculous and utterly inadequate in the face of life's overpowering difficulties, it also fails to reckon with the power and sovereignty of God. Imagine a slightly different story—in this case, a true story. In 1979, a 29-year-old woman jumped from the top of the Empire State building, and was on her way to certain death when a gust of wind blew her onto a window ledge. God saved that woman. In this case, he did it by using the 'ordinary', 'natural' means at his disposal. God needn't have done it that way—he could have suspended the laws of gravity if he had so chosen—but he chose to manipulate ordinary everyday means to achieve an extraordinary end.

Not many readers may subscribe exactly to Mr Barclay's view of prayer, but the assumption that lies behind his view is very widespread—that is, the assumption that the world is separated into the two categories of 'natural' and 'supernatural'. People turn God's habitual way of doing things into 'laws of nature' to which God is then bound.

This is not a biblical way of thinking. In the Bible, everything is under God's control; his powerful word sustains all things (Col 1:17; Heb 1:3). Remember the opening of Jeremiah's prayer: "Ah, Lord GOD! It is you who has made the heavens and the earth by your great power and by your outstretched arm! Nothing is too hard for you" (Jer 32:17). The God who is in complete control of his world in every place and at all times can do anything he pleases. He can use natural means to achieve natural results, such as simply sending the rain to water the earth and produce crops. He can use natural means to achieve extraordinary results—such as sending a strong east wind to drive back the Red Sea and allow the Israelites to cross on dry land (Exod 14:21). Or he can suspend the normal, natural pattern of his creation by bringing back to life a man who has been dead for four days (John 11:38-44). All are equally the work of the powerful, sovereign God of all the world.

However, if we accept the pagan (and very modern) separation of the world into 'natural' and 'supernatural', we very quickly find God parked off in the 'supernatural' realm, and he becomes merely an explanation for what science does not yet understand: the so-called 'God of the gaps'.

Christians who subconsciously adopt this way of thinking about God and the world can end up virtually prayerless. If, deep down, we don't think that God is actually able to act or intervene to change anything in our daily lives, but is only going to give us a bit of strength to put up with things as they are, then prayer doesn't seem so urgent or necessary. We can just get on with managing things ourselves, firing off the occasional brief request for some extra patience and perseverance.

This is a grave danger for modern Christians, especially those living in the prosperous West. We live in a materialist-dominated world, where most diseases seem easily curable and where life is, for the most part, secure, comfortable and healthy. If we don't take active steps to the contrary, our default way of thinking about the world will be that life goes on very normally without God—that he doesn't really do anything in the world anymore, and that his activity is limited to making us feel a bit better. At most, we might be driven to prayer in desperation when things fall apart. But our implicit, daily belief—reinforced by the media, the education system and our interaction with others—is that God is impotent to intervene and actually do anything of any significance in our world. He may have set the world going but he doesn't dabble in it much these days.

If we are wondering why our prayer lives might be ailing, perhaps it is because we are infected with this unbiblical way of thinking. Perhaps we have ceased to believe that God is supremely **able** to work in his world, through both normal everyday means and extraordinary inexplicable means. Perhaps we have developed a subtle scepticism about the limits of his power.

WE SAID AT THE BEGINNING OF THIS section that doubt in God's ability to act in his world came in two forms. We have looked at the first of these—that God is not really able to work because he is limited by the fixed natural laws of the world. The second form also places a limit on God's ability to act—in this case because of his fixed, unchangeable sovereign will. This view states that, if God is completely in control and has his plans for the world and for each one of us, then whatever else prayer might achieve, it cannot alter God's plans. God will do what God will do, whether we pray or not. Prayer may have beneficial effects on **us**, in increasing our daily trust in him for example, but it has no effect on God himself. Otherwise, how could God be sovereign?

We'll come back and talk further about how our prayers interact with God's sovereign will in chapter 8, but for the time being we simply need to note that this view of God and prayer is directly and repeatedly contradicted by Scripture. What does "You do not have, because you do not ask" mean in James 4:2 if God does not respond to our prayers by giving us things? Or what are we to make of the many instances in the Old Testament which speak of God 'relenting' in response to heartfelt prayers, and not visiting upon people the wrath and destruction he had intended (e.g. Exod 32:9-14; Jer 26:19; Joel 2:13)? Why would God promise us that we could "call upon me in the day of trouble; I will deliver you" (Ps 50:15) if our calling upon him had no effect—that is, if the outcome of the day of trouble would have been precisely the same, according to God's eternal will, whether we had prayed or not? And what do these words about Elijah mean if not that God acts in response to human prayers?

> The prayer of a righteous person has great power as it is working. Elijah was a man with a nature like ours, and he prayed fervently that it might not rain, and for three years and six months it did not rain on the earth. Then he prayed again, and heaven gave rain, and the earth bore its fruit. (James 5:16b-18)

The Bible certainly affirms the absolutely sovereignty and power of God over his creation at every moment, and his determination to work his plans and purposes out. But it never takes that to mean that God is deaf to our prayers—that they rebound without effect from the hard, shiny surface of his eternal decrees. Quite the contrary, Scripture everywhere assumes that God will graciously respond to his people's prayers and include their prayers in his plans. When we stop believing this, for whatever reason, we stop praying.

b. We question whether God is willing

Even if the effectiveness of prayer is granted and God's ability to act is accepted, there is still the problem of his **willingness** to act. For the Christian, this at first seems like a blasphemous suggestion. God not willing to act for our benefit? How preposterous!

However, we feel the emotional force of this question rather more acutely in the face of suffering. Why did God not intervene to stop the Asian tsunami? Why does my life continue to be dogged with illness and heartache? Why did he let my child die?

All this, of course, is part of a big and multi-faceted question, often described as the 'problem of evil'. We can't hope to do the subject justice in this short space, but we can note a few helpful points.[2]

For one thing, we shouldn't think that we're the first ones to struggle with this issue. The psalmists often cried out to God in a kind of spiritual agony, questioning what God was doing and why he seemed to delay in keeping his promises. In Psalm 89, for example, the psalmist just couldn't understand what was happening. God had made a covenant to establish David's throne forever but now that throne was lying in ruins, destroyed by Israel's enemies. What was God doing?

> But now you have cast off and rejected;
>> you are full of wrath against your anointed.
> You have renounced the covenant with your servant;
>> you have defiled his crown in the dust.
> You have breached all his walls;
>> you have laid his strongholds in ruins ...
> How long, O LORD? Will you hide yourself forever?
>> How long will your wrath burn like fire? ...

---

2   For a short but useful treatment of the subject, read John Dickson's, *If I were God, I'd end all the pain* (Matthias Media, Kingsford, 2001). For a more detailed theological discussion of the issues, try Don Carson's *How Long, O Lord?* (Baker, Grand Rapids, 1990).

Lord, where is your steadfast love of old,
    which by your faithfulness you swore to David?
Remember, O Lord, how your servants are mocked,
    and how I bear in my heart the insults of all the
        many nations,
with which your enemies mock, O Lord,
    with which they mock the footsteps of your
        anointed.
Blessed be the Lord forever!
    Amen and Amen. (Ps 89:38-40, 46, 49-52)

The psalmist certainly doesn't hold back. Where are you, Lord? What are you doing? Don't you love us any more? Has your faithfulness run out? Look at how everyone makes fun of us because we trust you, and makes fun of you because you seem so powerless!

And at the close of this anguished prayer there is no resolution or answer, no indication that God has heard or acted. There is simply the cry, "Blessed be the Lord forever!"

It reminds us of the sorrowful prayer of Jesus in the Garden of Gethsemane as he wrestled with the awful consequences of God's will for him: "Abba, Father, all things are possible for you. Remove this cup from me. Yet not what I will, but what you will" (Mark 14:36).

Three times he prays this heartfelt prayer. And God's answer comes almost immediately. Judas arrives with an armed mob and Jesus says, "See, the hour is at hand, and the Son of Man is betrayed into the hands of sinners" (Matt 26:45).

In the cross of Christ, we see the problem of evil focused to a shining point of light. How could God let this happen? How could he allow his own Son, the sinless Son of Man, be betrayed and mocked and beaten and killed? Where is God's justice? Where is God's protection? Why does God sit on his hands and do nothing, letting this monstrous evil unfold? "Abba, Father, all things are possible for you", says Jesus in Mark's version of his prayer. God is quite able to intervene and prevent Jesus' arrest, as Jesus himself reminds Peter: "Do you think that I cannot appeal to my Father, and he will at once send me more than twelve legions of angels?" (Matt 26:53). So why doesn't he? Why doesn't God send in the angelic cavalry? Why is he unwilling to save his own beloved Son from a cruel, unjust death?

The answer that blasts out from the rest of the New Testament is that it was God's grand, gracious, glorious plan that his Son would suffer and die, the righteous for the unrighteous, to bring us to himself (1 Pet 3:18). Jesus may have been mistreated and killed by the Jewish authorities with the help of the Romans, but God was really behind the whole thing: "this Jesus, delivered up according to the definite plan and foreknowledge of God, you crucified and killed by the hands of lawless men" (Acts 2:23).

In other words, God achieves his plans, not only in spite of human opposition and sin, and in spite of evil, but **through** all these things. Sin and evil do not thwart his plans. On the contrary, he is able to work in and through the evil that we do in order to achieve his good purposes. We see this again and again in the Bible— for example, when Joseph says to his lying, treacherous brothers, "you meant evil against me, but God meant it for good ..." (Gen 50:20).

We don't always see or understand what the 'good' is that God is achieving through the evil circumstances of life. That perception may come with time, such as when we look back and see how much our faith has grown as a result of some particularly trying experience. Or we may never perceive what it was that God was doing until all is revealed on the Last Day.

Whether we can catch a glimpse of the good that God is bringing out of the evil or not, the godly response is exemplified by Jesus: "Yet not what I will, but what you will". The godly response is not "Why did God ...?" or "Why didn't God ...?" but "How can I respond in trust and obedience in this situation? What is God teaching me in this?"

We find this hard, of course. We know that God is trustworthy, and that we should not doubt him. But we doubt him all the same. We fall victim, not to the problem of evil, but to the age-old problem of sin. Right from the beginning, Satan has been tempting mankind to doubt the goodness and generosity of God. His strategy with Eve was to sow doubt in her mind about God's good intentions (Gen 3:1-5). And so it is with us. When things go wrong, the thoughts immediately rise in our minds: "Why is he doing this to me? Does he really have my best interests at heart? Or am I just a pawn in his cosmic game of chess? I keep praying but I just don't get an answer. Nothing seems to change. If he is so powerful and so loving, why doesn't he answer me?"

At these times, we need to remind ourselves of God's absolute goodness and faithfulness, shown through all creation throughout history, and shown especially in the death of the Lord Jesus:

> He who did not spare his own Son but gave him up
> for us all, how will he not also with him graciously
> give us all things? (Rom 8:32)

We also need to remind ourselves that the answer we are looking for from God may not be the answer that he gives. The Bible promises that God does hear and answer. It's just that he may not answer in quite the way we expect. His answer may be "No".

A FURTHER WAY IN WHICH WE doubt God's willingness to answer our prayers is that we think our requests may be too small or insignificant to warrant his attention. Why would a God who is so big and powerful and majestic be interested in my trivial prayer about Aunty Edie's ingrown toenail? Why would the mighty Lord of the Universe be bothered with responding to my request for help in the exams tomorrow? How could God be interested in all the details of our lives?

The answer is that God is so powerful and mighty

and sovereign, and so loving and gracious and kind, that he listens and responds even to the smallest most insignificant request. Jesus expresses this detailed care that God has for his people in his famous saying about hair and sparrows:

> "Are not two sparrows sold for a penny? And not one of them will fall to the ground apart from your Father. But even the hairs of your head are all numbered. Fear not, therefore; you are of more value than many sparrows." (Matt 10:29-31)

We need not worry that God is too busy to listen, or think that our prayers have to reach a certain threshold of importance or urgency before he will bother with them. Indeed, he is able to do far more than we can ask or imagine (Eph 3:20).

2. False views of relationship with God

Not only do we absorb false ideas or get confused about God himself, we also often accumulate false understandings about our **relationship** with God. Just as our relationship with God is one of the glorious reasons why we can pray (see chapter 3), so a false understanding of how we relate to God, and he to us, can pour cold water over the fires of our prayer lives.

This problem comes in many forms. Let us look at just a few.

a. Faith and disobedience

Our relationship with God is based on trust (i.e. 'faith'). God is faithful and dependable, and we rely on him. We trust that his words are true, that he forgives us through the atoning death of his Son, and that he loves us and is working at all times for our good.

Prayer is a verbal expression of this trust. As we ask God for things, we are giving voice to our dependence on him for everything.

But trust in God is not only about depending upon him to care for us and provide for us; it also includes trusting his words and commands and instructions for our lives. Trust in God means hearing God say, "Do not lie", and believing him when he tells us that we must not do this, both for our good and for the good of others.

This is why the opposite of faith in the Bible is not simply unbelief or faithlessness, but disobedience. This comes out in Hebrews 3 where the author reminds his readers of how Israel rebelled against God in the wilderness by refusing to go up and take possession of the promised land:

> As it is said,
>
> > "Today, if you hear his voice,
> > do not harden your hearts as in the rebellion."
>
> For who were those who heard and yet rebelled? Was it not all those who left Egypt led by Moses?

And with whom was he provoked for forty years?
Was it not with those who sinned, whose bodies fell
in the wilderness? And to whom did he swear that
they would not enter his rest, but to those who were
disobedient? So we see that they were unable to
enter because of unbelief. (Heb 3:15-19)

Notice that unbelief and disobedience are virtually the same thing in this passage. Israel wouldn't accept God's word that he would help them conquer the land, and so they rebelled and disobeyed him. Their unbelief was disobedience.

Just as trust is the lifeblood of prayer, so disobedience makes prayer virtually impossible, for when we are disobedient, we are expressing unbelief not faith. We should not think that our lifestyle and attitudes are somehow partitioned off from our prayer lives. When the relationship is foundering (through persistent disobedience), the only prayer left to us is one of repentance.

If we are rebelling against God and refusing to repent of our disobedience, we will not want to come to him in prayer; nor should we think that he will listen to us if we did. As God says to Israel:

"When you spread out your hands,
    I will hide my eyes from you;
even though you make many prayers,
    I will not listen;
    your hands are full of blood." (Isa 1:15)

b. Results and ritual

It is quite common for people to think that we can only be sure that our prayers have been heard by God when we receive what we ask for. This is also a misunderstanding of our relationship with him. God is not a cosmic butler, always snapping to attention and following our orders. This is not how we relate to him or he to us.

God promises that he hears us when we pray, whether or not he grants our requests. This again is a matter of trust. Do we believe God when he assures us of his attention to our prayers, even if we don't get the results we hoped for?

There is a further danger here. If we link good 'results' with God hearing us, then it is only a very short step to thinking that it must have been something about the way we prayed on that particular occasion that prompted God to listen and act. We pray again that way in the hope that it will again achieve a result. Before long, we have replaced genuine, open relationship with God with a mechanistic ritual designed to achieve maximum results—that is, to manipulate God into acting as we want him to.

When we mention 'ritual', we immediately think of elaborate church services, robes and candles. But ritual comes in domestic versions too. It is sometimes tempting to think that our morning quiet time is an insurance policy against a bad day ("If your day is hemmed with prayer it is less likely to unravel", as the old poster put it). Or we invest particular postures or forms of words with special power for getting things done (*The Prayer of Jabez* comes to mind).[3]

Of course, ritual is not wrong in itself. Using familiar structures and forms can be helpful. However, if we start to think that our little rituals somehow impress God and ensure the success of our prayers, we have denied the true nature of our relationship with him. That relationship is all about his goodness and grace and our humble trust, not about 'results'.

c. Faith in feelings

We have also misunderstood our relationship with God if we think that feelings are its key barometer. Our relationship with God is an objective fact, but our feelings vary widely from hour to hour in response to all kinds of stimuli (some spiritual, some worldly, some dietary!).

Remember, 'faith' is not a mysterious religious feeling or quality; it is trust, reliance and dependence on God. And the important thing about trust is not how strong the trust is or how it feels, but whether the thing you're trusting in is trustworthy!

---

[3] Bruce Wilkinson, *The Prayer of Jabez: Breaking Through to the Blessed Life*, Multnomah, Sisters, 2000.

Do you think you are less of a Christian when you feel sad or low or discouraged? Or do you think you are less of a Christian when you are sick or suffering or tired? If you do, then perhaps what you are really trusting in or relying upon is not Christ himself but the quality of your 'faith'. This is a relatively common mistake. It's not our faith that gets us right with God and saves us; it is Christ who saves us through his atoning death and glorious resurrection. He has done the work. Our job is simply to trust in his incredible trustworthiness. How this feels will change from day to day. But Jesus Christ does not change—he is the same yesterday and today and forever (Heb 13:8).

The same is true of prayer, which is a verbal expression of our faith. Sometimes we will feel very much like praying. Sometimes we won't. Sometimes prayer feels sweet and delightful; at other times, it feels like a wrestling match; and at other times, we feel as if the heavens are silent and distant, and that our prayers are going nowhere.

These feelings are natural and common, but they are no indication of the quality of our prayers or the extent to which God has heard them. Indeed, if we wait until we feel like praying, some of us might never pray again.

If prayer is the vocal expression of our relationship with God and that relationship is based on truth and reality (like Christ's death and my decision to trust in it), then prayer, too, is to be an objective fact of our experience, not a subjective impression of our feelings.

3. God, Satan and prayer

Why is it, then, that we do not pray? The real basis of our difficulty is not intellectual; it is moral and spiritual. We fail to pray, primarily, because of our sin and because the Enemy does not want us to pray.

Prayer, at its heart, is an acknowledgment of need. It expresses our frailty and dependence, and our desire for help. This acknowledgment is hard for sinful human beings. It brings us low. It forces us to admit that we are not independent or self-sufficient—two lies that are very dear to us. And Satan, the Father of Lies, wants us to keep believing them. He wants us to stand tall and go it alone, not humbly kneel and express our dependence on God for everything.

There are two very interesting passages in the New Testament which refer to resisting Satan, and both are in the context of prayer:

> Submit yourselves therefore to God. Resist the devil, and he will flee from you. Draw near to God, and he will draw near to you. (Jas 4:7-8)

> Humble yourselves, therefore, under the mighty hand of God so that at the proper time he may exalt you, casting all your anxieties on him, because he cares for you. Be sober-minded; be watchful. Your adversary the devil prowls around like a roaring lion, seeking someone to devour. (1 Pet 5:6-8)

Every Christian has experienced this in some way. You

start to pray and immediately the busyness of life seems to intensify. The phone rings, the children demand your attention, some pressing work commitments spring to mind and your good intentions of prayer evaporate. Or else the thought arises in your mind, "I just don't feel like praying now. Perhaps I'll try again later when I'm more in the mood."

Nor are the distractions and obstacles to prayer that Satan puts in our way always immediate and short-term. Sometimes life is one big distraction. Many modern people live lives of such incessant activity and busyness that there is little time or energy for prayer. We swallow Satan's lie that if we just work harder and run faster, we will achieve all our goals and live happily ever after. "Do more, achieve more, have more, watch more, experience more", he whispers in our ears (sometimes through his minions in the advertising industry). And we duly fill our lives with ever more distractions.

If we are 'too busy to pray', then we must repent of our over-activism and resist Satan's attempts to distract us into prayerlessness. We must act on the promise of God that if we stand against the Adversary's attacks, then Satan will flee and God will draw near to us.

The Garden of Gethsemane is a compelling illustration of all this (see Mark 14:32-50). Jesus tells the disciples to watch and pray so that they will not fall into temptation. They fall asleep and, when temptation comes (in the form of Judas and the soldiers), they deny Jesus and flee.

Jesus, however, keeps praying. Temptation comes to him also, but he does not falter. He prays earnestly for deliverance from his impending death but he does not get what he asks for. And yet, through prayer, he resists the Evil One and continues faithfully along the agonizing road to the Cross.

In seeking to emulate Jesus, the hardest part is starting. It is easier, in many ways, to keep praying than to start praying. Luke 18:1-8 (the persistent widow) and Luke 11:5-13 (the friend at midnight) are usually taken as exhortations to persevere in prayer. Both passages, in fact, are encouragements to start praying. They are parables of contrast rather than comparison. If even sinful humans accede to persistent demands, how much more will our gracious God grant us every good gift—and speedily.

When we pray, we know that God draws near to us. We know this because he promises to and his words are utterly trustworthy. Sometimes, the hardest part is starting.

Chapter 5

HOW TO PRAY

"GOOD", YOU MAY BE THINKING. "At last we're getting down to the nitty-gritty. Enough of the theory and the motivation. Give me some practical advice. Tell me how to do it!"

You may be surprised to find that the Bible really doesn't say very much at all about **how** to pray. There aren't detailed instructions about whether we should sit, stand or kneel. There are no set times or places; there is no set form of words or formula that we should repeat. No techniques are taught to get us 'in the mood' or to make it more likely that our prayer will be answered.

Given what we have seen so far about the nature of prayer and the God we pray to, none of this should be strange or surprising. God is not a piece of software that we program in a certain way in order to get a certain result. Nor is he an impersonal force or power that we get in touch with through mystical techniques, such as chanting or fasting. God is personal and we relate to him through speech. We don't relate to God through a series of 'techniques' any more than we relate to our spouses or children or friends that way.

1. God's voice and ours

One very obvious biblical 'how to' is that prayer is verbal. It's made up of words, spoken by us to God. This may seem like a rather simplistic or even unnecessary point to make, but it still needs to be made, especially given how often it is challenged.

For example, it is quite common for people to say that prayer is just as much a matter of 'listening to God' as speaking to him. In his well-known little book on prayer, *Too busy not to pray*, Bill Hybels says,

> ... as I've studied prayer and prayed, I've sensed God saying, "If we enjoy a relationship, why are you doing all the talking? Let *me* get a word in somewhere!"[1]

And he proceeds to spend Part III of the book discussing the whole subject of how we listen to God in prayer.

---

[1] B. Hybels, *Too busy not to pray*, IVP, Downers Grove, 1989, pp. 107-108.

In one sense, Bill Hybels is quite right; listening to God is a vital element of our relationship with him. In fact, we can only have a relationship with God in the first place by listening to his word—the gospel—and responding to it. As Charles Wesley's famous hymn says,

> He speaks; and listening to his voice,
> new life the dead receive;
> the mournful broken hearts rejoice;
> the humble poor believe.[2]

The Christian life starts as we hear God's voice and respond in faith, and it continues in the same way. Our daily, life-giving spiritual food is to listen to every word that proceeds from the mouth of God as his Spirit applies the Scriptures to our hearts (Matt 4:4). Listening to God is the basis of all that we do and think. It is essential. It's just that 'prayer' is the wrong word to describe it.

In the Bible, prayer is not listening to God's voice; it is **responding to God's voice** by presenting our requests before him. This is what we saw in chapter 3, 'Why pray?' We pray because God has initiated a relationship with us through the gospel, because he has commanded us to pray, and because he has made very great and precious promises to hear us and to give us every good

---

[2]   Verse 5 of 'O for a thousand tongues to sing', 1739. (Appears as verse 4 in some versions of the hymn.)

gift. We speak to God because God first speaks to us. (Indeed, as a practical point, many Christians begin their prayer-times with Bible reading so that their prayers are shaped by God and his word.) Listening to God's voice is vital. We just shouldn't confuse it with 'prayer'.

Much the same confusion surrounds the subject of meditation. There is such a thing as 'meditation' in the Bible. It is not the mystical trance of Eastern mysticism, in which the mind is emptied through various exercises, such as the repetitive chanting of a word or sound. In the Bible, meditation is not emptying the mind, but filling it—with the word of God. It is thinking about God and his law; dwelling upon his character and deeds; mulling over his goodness and greatness; reminding ourselves about his promises and faithfulness. As the psalmist repeatedly says in Psalm 119,

> Oh how I love your law!
>   It is my meditation all the day. (Ps 119:97)

And as the LORD says to Joshua,

> "This Book of the Law shall not depart from your
> mouth, but you shall meditate on it day and night,
> so that you may be careful to do according to all that
> is written in it. For then you will make your way
> prosperous, and then you will have good success."
> (Josh 1:8)

Biblical meditation is an important practice. It is perhaps the closest thing we see in the Bible to our modern habit of daily Bible reading. And biblical meditation is a powerful stimulus to prayer. But it is not prayer.

Prayer is asking God for things. And as we have seen already, it has this character because of the personal God to whom we pray, and because of how he has created us.

2. Time and posture

For these reasons, we need to be careful about saying too much about the right times and postures for prayer.

The best time for prayer is **any time and at all times** —in good times, in bad times, in flat times and boring times. There's no law that says, "No prayer, no breakfast", although praying first thing in the morning is an excellent habit. There's also no inherent advantage in praying at night as opposed to at midday, or in praying for hours as opposed to minutes. We are not to be like the pagans Jesus criticizes in Matthew 6 who "think that they will be heard for their many words", as if God is slow to hear us or to understand what we need. Nor should we imagine that he is more likely to bend and grant our requests if we really put ourselves out by praying in the middle of the night.

Of course there's nothing wrong with praying at **any** time or for any length of time. Jesus himself "went out to the mountain to pray, and all night he continued in prayer to God" (Luke 6:12). Oh that our problem was that we kept praying for too long!

But we mustn't fall into the trap of thinking that our efforts in prayer **merit** an answer from God. An all-night prayer vigil is no more or less likely to be heard and answered by God than the Lord's Prayer, which takes less than a minute to pray. God hears and answers our prayers because of his gracious kindness. He is not only willing and ready to give us good gifts but, through the gospel, he has granted us access to his throne. He hears and answers because of his goodness and grace in Christ Jesus, not because he is so mightily impressed with the quality or length of our prayers.

The same can be said about posture. There is no law that says prayer must take place on our knees. Standing, sitting or even walking are all fine. Some people in the Bible pray flat on their faces—though, for some of us, lying down to pray may not be the best posture, unless we want to have a particularly quiet 'quiet time'.

Having said that, there **is** a posture of prayer that God himself recommends. It is described in Isaiah 66:

> Thus says the LORD:
> "Heaven is my throne,
>   and the earth is my footstool;
> what is the house that you would build for me,
>   and what is the place of my rest?
> All these things my hand has made,
>   and so all these things came to be,
>   declares the LORD.

But this is the one to whom I will look:
>   he who is humble and contrite in spirit
>   and trembles at my word." (Isa 66:1-2)

David says much the same thing in Psalm 51:

> The sacrifices of God are a broken spirit;
>   a broken and contrite heart, O God, you will not
>   despise. (Ps 51:17)

We are all sinners and we remain sinners throughout our lives. We might be tempted to minimize the problem, rationalize it, make excuses for it or comfort ourselves by looking at other more blatant offenders. Indeed, long-time Christians often find it easy to go through the motions of Christian living, avoiding heinous sins and gradually becoming blind to the deep-seated corruption and selfishness in their own hearts.

We need to keep hearing the Bible's reminder: "The heart is deceitful above all things, and desperately sick; who can understand it?" (Jer 17:9). Our experience bears this out. We keep doing things that we can't understand, that we know are wrong and that we don't really want to do at all. Even in our better moments, our motives are a strange mixture of godliness, selfishness and pride.

Thus the true posture for prayer is repentance and humility. We approach the holy God in prayer only through his grace to us in Jesus Christ.

3. The essence of how

This brings us to the essence of how we pray to God. As we've already seen, God is an able, fatherly, listening, holy and merciful God, and, through the gospel of Christ, he becomes **our** Father. That is, although we are selfish and rebellious by nature and we don't want to depend upon him (and therefore we don't want to pray), all the same he sends his Son into the world to die as a ransom for many and to rise as Messiah to pour out his Spirit on his people, granting us repentance and forgiveness of sins, and a new eternal relationship with God as our Father.

This is the core—the heart—the foundation of prayer. What the Bible says about **how** we should pray all flows from this. Let's look at it under six headings.

a. We pray as dependent sons

The Lord's Prayer begins with two of the most extraordinary words in the whole Bible: "Our Father". We glide straight past this momentous statement as if it were obvious or normal, but it is neither. That the God we pray to is a 'father' is glorious enough, but that he should be **our** Father and thus that we should be his children—this is simply too wonderful.

J. I. Packer described the blessing of adoption as "the highest privilege that the gospel offers".[3] This is

---

[3]   J. I. Packer, *Knowing God*, Hodder & Stoughton, London, 1973, p. 230.

no exaggeration. Through the saving death and resurrection of Jesus, God the Father meets our most basic spiritual need. He freely justifies us, pardoning our sins, declaring us righteous and assuring us that we are safe from his judgement because of the atoning sacrifice of Christ. But the spiritual blessing of the gospel goes even beyond this free justification. On the basis of our justification, we are called and welcomed into his own family as his adopted sons. We are no longer enemies, but family; no longer slaves, but sons. As Galatians 4 says:

> But when the fullness of time had come, God sent forth his Son, born of woman, born under the law, to redeem those who were under the law, so that we might receive adoption as sons. And because you are sons, God has sent the Spirit of his Son into our hearts, crying, "Abba! Father!" So you are no longer a slave, but a son, and if a son, then an heir through God. (Gal 4:4-7)

As adopted sons, we need have no fear or embarrassment about coming before our Father to make our requests of him. We need not cringe with fear or think that he does not really want us to bother him. He loves us to come to him and call on him, expressing our dependence upon him for everything. And we should not doubt his willingness to hear and answer. For if human fathers are more than willing to listen to their children's requests, and won't give them a stone when they ask for bread, how much more will our heavenly Father grant good things to those who ask him (Matt 7:9-11)?

Thinking of ourselves as adopted sons helps us avoid two errors. On the one hand, it prevents us being unwilling to come to the Father because of our feelings of shame or unworthiness. Our adoption as God's sons assures us of the Father's care and concern for us, and his constant attentiveness to our prayers. On the other hand, our adoption also deflates any pride or presumption we might have in approaching God, as if somehow he were bound to follow our orders and do whatever we say. We are **adoptive** sons —we deserve nothing from God but judgement and yet, by his incredible grace, we can approach him and make known our requests.

Adopted sons come before the heavenly Father with confidence and boldness, yet also with humility and respect. We know both the depth of our unworthiness, and his boundless mercy and goodness.

The Bible's word for this attitude of humble confidence is 'faith' which, as we've seen before, simply means reliance, trust and dependence. Prayer is just audible faith. It's the attitude of humble dependence expressing itself in words as we make our requests to God our Father.

b. We pray by the Spirit

The second important thing to say about **how** we pray is that it is in and by the Holy Spirit—which is another way of saying that we only pray because God enables us to.

Left to ourselves, we couldn't pray. After all, by nature we are rebels against God. By nature, we are spiritually dead, "following the course of this world, following the prince of the power of the air, the spirit that is now at work in the sons of disobedience", as Paul puts it (Eph 2:2). Without God's intervention, we have a very different spirit at work within us.

But such is the kindness and grace and power of God that he not only sent his Son to redeem us, he also sends out his Spirit to breathe new life into us. It is God's Spirit who works within us to convict our consciences of our own guilt and the marvellous truth of the gospel (John 16:8), and who enables us to confess Christ Jesus as Lord (1 Cor 12:3; cf. 1 John 4:2-3).

In other words, it is only by the secret operation of God's Spirit stirring and reviving our dead hearts that we turn to him in the first place and put our trust in Christ. As we do so, God pours out his Spirit upon us, baptizing us in him (1 Cor 12:12-13), washing and renewing us (Tit 3:5-7), and guaranteeing us that we are indeed citizens of heaven with an eternal inheritance in store (Eph 1:13-14; 2 Cor 1:22). In giving us his Spirit, God himself comes to dwell with us and in us. The Spirit is not a separate bit of God; he is the Spirit of the Father and of the Son. And so when the Spirit is poured out richly upon us, the Father and the Son come to make their home with us (John 14:16-17, 23; cf. Rom 8:9-11).

The Holy Spirit's initial work in our lives is to convict us of sin, and to renew and regenerate our dead hearts. He opens our eyes to see Jesus as our Lord and God as our Father. His ongoing work is to lead us into holiness—to prompt and urge and empower us to become more like God's Son (Rom 8:28-29). Under the Spirit's leadership, we put to death all that belongs to our old life, and we bring forth the fruit of righteousness and good character in our lives (see Rom 8:12-14; Gal 5:16-25).

Here's the connection with prayer: **in leading and empowering us to become like the Son, the Spirit testifies to us that we are sons too!** This is the meaning of what at first seems a rather complicated passage in Romans 8. Look closely at what Paul says:

> [13] For if you live according to the flesh you will die, but if by the Spirit you put to death the deeds of the body, you will live. [14] For all who are led by the Spirit of God are sons of God. [15] For you did not receive the spirit of slavery to fall back into fear, but you have received the Spirit of adoption as sons, by whom we cry, "Abba! Father!" [16] The Spirit himself bears witness with our spirit that we are children of God, [17] and if children, then heirs—heirs of God and fellow heirs with Christ, provided we suffer with him in order that we may also be glorified with him. (Rom 8:13-17)

The argument goes like this:

- vv. 13-14: By the Spirit, we put to death the misdeeds of the body. This is the same as saying that we are "led by the Spirit of God" (see the connection between verses 13 and 14).
- v. 14: All those who are led by the Spirit of God are sons of God; we therefore know that we are sons of God because God's Spirit is leading us to put to death the misdeeds of the body.
- v. 15: It could not be otherwise because we did not receive a 'spirit' that would lead us back into the slavery of ungodliness, but God's own Spirit as his sons, so that we cry out to him as Father.
- vv. 16-17: So there are two 'spirits' that testify that we are God's sons. One is that we ourselves in our spirit now call out to him as Father, having been brought to new life, and knowing that we are justified and adopted into his family through the redemption that is in Christ Jesus. Alongside our own spirit is the testimony from the Holy Spirit himself who, by leading us to put to death the misdeeds of the body, shows that we are God's own sons.

In other words, God's work in our lives by his Spirit, leading us into godliness, is a marvellous testimony that we are God's own children who can approach him at any time to ask for his help. By the Spirit, we have passed from death to life—from hostility and enmity towards God, to sonship and peace with God. And because of the work of this same Spirit, we call out to God as our Father in prayer. Christian prayer can only take place "in the Spirit" (compare Eph 2:1-6, 14-17; 6:18).

c. We pray through the Son

We have already dwelt on the fact that, through the atoning work of the Lord Jesus Christ, we can become adopted sons of God and approach his throne with humble confidence. Christian prayer can only take place **through** the Lord Jesus Christ.

Paul puts it like this in his first letter to Timothy: "For there is one God, and there is one mediator between God and men, the man Christ Jesus, who gave himself as a ransom for all …" (1 Tim 2:5-6). A mediator is someone who stands between two hostile parties and makes peace. A mediator is a go-between—a bridge between two people or groups who are at war or who are in some way unacceptable to each other. Paul's point is that there are two parties: the one and only God, and humanity. And there is only one go-between who brings the two together, "the man Christ Jesus", who is both God and man, and who "gave himself as a ransom for all". God provided his own Son as the mediator—the one who would reconcile a hostile and sinful humanity to himself.

This is important to note because in Christian history it has been all too common to interpose

other mediators between God and man. Roman Catholicism, for example, suggests that we should pray through Mary or through particularly holy Christians who have died (whom they call 'saints'). This is not only entirely unnecessary, it is blasphemous. There is nothing lacking whatsoever in the quality of Jesus' sacrifice or his work as mediator, such that we need other mediators to help bring our prayers to God's attention. Mary was a humble, godly woman, but sinful like the rest of mankind. She knew her own need of a saviour and mediator before God (Luke 1:47).

The glory of the gospel is that we need no other human mediators to bring us to God—not Mary, not the saints, not the Church, not priests, not popes, not spiritual gurus or miracle workers, not anyone! For there is no other name under heaven by which we must be saved (Acts 4:12).

We must pray, then, through the Son and only through him.

d. We pray to the Father
The fourth thing to notice about how we pray is also something that we have touched on before—that prayer is directed to God the Father. This is the characteristic form of prayer in the New Testament, beginning with the Lord's Prayer (Matt 6:9) and Jesus' own prayers. The one we pray to is the Father in heaven, who is both willing and able to help in all

things, who cares for and sustains all things, and who longs to give good gifts to his children.

It is not wrong, of course, to pray to the Lord Jesus Christ. In fact there are a couple of examples in the New Testament of people calling out to the risen Jesus. As he is about to die, Stephen cries out, "Lord Jesus, receive my spirit" (Acts 7:59) and at the very end of 1 Corinthians, Paul begs Jesus, "Our Lord, come!" (1 Cor 16:22; cf. Rev 22:20).

Nor could you say that it would be wrong to pray to the Holy Spirit, since he is God—although there is no reference in the Bible to anyone praying to the Spirit.

However, the biblical pattern is to pray **to** the Father, **through** the Son, **by** the Spirit.

e. We pray with thanksgiving

Because of what God has done for us—because of his fatherly goodness in creation and because he redeems and saves us through Christ—thanksgiving should always be on our lips. Prayer without thanksgiving is like apple pie without ice-cream, or fish without chips. Thanksgiving is the perfect accompaniment to prayer because it acknowledges right up front how good God is, how marvellously he blesses us, and how graciously and constantly he listens and answers from heaven.

When Paul urges the Philippians not to be anxious about anything but in everything to make their requests known to God, he adds that it should be

with thanksgiving (Phil 4:6). This is absolutely typical of the Bible and of the Apostle Paul. Hardly a letter of his begins without an extended thanksgiving to God for all that God has done for the Christians to whom Paul is writing, and hardly a prayer of ours should begin without us pouring out our gratitude to the Father for all his blessings. "We ought always to give thanks to God for you, brothers, as is right", says Paul in the opening words of 2 Thessalonians.

f. We pray with difficulty

You may have been reading this chapter up to this point and thinking, "Well that all sounds well and fine. Inspiring, even. But you don't know what I'm like. You don't know how hard I find it to pray, how easily I'm distracted, how often I just get on with my day and forget all about God. What you're saying about prayer is true, I'm sure, but why is it so hard to put into practice?"

This is an important question, and one that causes heartache and uncertainty among many Christians. For if prayer is really 'audible faith'—if it is a basic and essential expression of our relationship with God— what does it say about me that I don't pray? Does it mean that I'm not really Christian at all?

The answer, of course, may be yes. The New Testament is quite clear that persistent, unrepentant sinfulness is an indication that someone has not really repented and put their faith in Christ. "Do not be deceived", says Paul, "neither the sexually immoral, nor idolaters, nor adulterers, nor men who practice homosexuality, nor thieves, nor the greedy, nor drunkards, nor revilers, nor swindlers will inherit the kingdom of God" (1 Cor 6:9-10). And we might well add to the list "those who continually and stubbornly fail to give thanks to God and depend upon him in prayer".

If prayer plays no part in our lives—if we sail along in a state of blissful self-sufficiency, stopping neither to thank God nor to come before our Father in confession and prayer—then we are right to question the state of our souls. The right response is to stop and turn around—to repent, to put all our trust in the Lord Jesus Christ, and to express this trust by praying.

However, as we saw in chapter 4, we shouldn't be surprised that prayer is difficult. We remain sinners, even though we are forgiven and justified through Christ. The world continues to infect our minds with false ideas about God and our relationship with him. And our enemy the Devil also conspires against our prayers. Given all this opposition, it is no wonder that we continue to find prayer unnatural and difficult, even now that we have become adopted sons of our heavenly Father. It is no different from any other area of godliness. It is not natural and easy to be patient, loving, gracious and good. The battle rages throughout our Christian lives:

> But I say, walk by the Spirit, and you will not gratify
> the desires of the flesh. For the desires of the flesh

are against the Spirit, and the desires of the Spirit are against the flesh, for these are opposed to each other, to keep you from doing the things you want to do. (Gal 5:16-17)

If we want to pray but are struggling to keep at it, we can be comforted by the fact that this is entirely what the Bible would lead us to expect. Situation normal. This reassurance doesn't reduce the urgency and importance of continuing in prayer—as Paul says, "But I say, walk by the Spirit"—but it does protect us from despair. With determination and hope we can, like Epaphras, continue to struggle and wrestle in prayer (Col 4:12).

4. How then do we pray?

The Bible is not very big on technique when it comes to prayer because ultimately prayer is based on and expresses a **relationship** with God as our Father, and relationships don't tend to work by technique. All the same, by thinking further about our relationship with God (which is basically what we have done in this chapter), we have learnt some important lessons about how to pray. We've learnt that we should pray with humble confidence in God as our Father, bringing our requests to him in the name of Jesus Christ the Son, through the working of the Spirit within us. We should also saturate our prayers with thankfulness for all God's goodness and kindness to us. And we should keep on struggling and wrestling in our prayers, realizing that it will be difficult to persevere in prayer, and asking for God's help and strength as we do so.

As for the practicalities of how we pray—whether we pray out loud, silently in our minds or even write down our prayers; whether we pray in the morning or at night or in between; whether or not we read a passage of Scripture first to stimulate our thoughts; whether we use prayer lists and diaries or just pray for the people and issues that are on our minds—all these things are matters of freedom.

The experience of most Christians is that habit and novelty are both important in prayer. We need to set aside time to pray (or else it usually gets squeezed out) and, for most people, having a normal time each day when they pray works best. There is no law about this, as if the Bible says somewhere that "thou shalt do a 20-minute quiet time every day". However, given that we are sinful people who are prone to finding reasons not to pray, having a certain time set aside each day can help remind and prompt us to pray. We should also remember that, while Christianity does not mandate daily set times for prayer (like Islam, for example), we are commanded to "pray without ceasing" (1 Thess 5:17) and to "be constant in prayer" (Rom 12:12). If we assert our freedom from law by praying only irregularly and occasionally, are we obeying this command from the Lord? God calls us to far more than set daily devotions at particular hours of the day; he urges and invites us to pray every day and any day, at all times and at any time, for two minutes or two hours. The routine we develop and the length of time for which we pray are not significant. What is important is that we constantly and continually express our trust and confidence in God by calling upon him in prayer.

For most people, novelty is just as important as regularity in prayer. Praying in exactly the same way, in the same pattern or with the same words becomes stale after a while. Some variety in the way we approach prayer is usually helpful. (For some further practical suggestions, see question 2 in chapter 10.)

Again, we need to keep reminding ourselves that 'technique' is not the essence of prayer—as if, by hitting upon the right method or system, all our problems will be over and prayer will be the easiest and most natural thing in the world. Prayer is not a matter of technique but of relationship.

Chapter 6

THE DESIRES OF GOD

IMAGINE YOURSELF IN THE ceiling cavity of an old holiday cottage near the beach, trying to plug a leak in the roof. It is 2 am. Heavy rain is beating down. Your wife is trying to arrange buckets to catch the water that is still dripping steadily onto the bed, while sweetly inquiring as to your progress.

It occurs to you that it would not be a bad time to pray. But what to pray for? Of course you pray for the rain to stop—immediately. This feels a little bit selfish —even self-indulgent—until you remember the Beach Mission team that is camping on the other side of the lake. Surely, as an act of selfless concern for the brave missioners, you can plead for the rain to cease?

Then you think of the farmers in the local area who

have been longing for rain these past 12 months. Perhaps you should pray that the rain continues for days for their sake. Or maybe the best compromise is to ask that God suspends his normal practice of sending rain on the "just and on the unjust" alike (Matt 5:45), and gives the farmers a soaking while keeping the Beach Mission team (and coincidentally your holiday cottage) dry.

We often don't know what to pray for. When a close relative is sick and dying, riddled with cancer, do we continue to pray for healing, or do we pray for a quick and merciful death? Should we pray that God would give us this job or that job, or this house or that house? Or is it rather too tacky and selfish to be praying about any of these sorts of things in the first place? How specific should we be in praying for particular things? Is it better to pray a kind of blanket prayer over everything: "Dear God, just do whatever you think is best. Amen"?

Then there is the problem of what we might call 'going blank'—that common experience of settling down to pray and then finding ourselves unable to think of anything much to pray about. We mumble a few familiar phrases and prayer requests—for wisdom, for safety, for blessings on our family, perhaps—and then our prayer peters out through lack of content.

Does the Bible offer any help in knowing what to pray for? Thankfully, yes.

As we saw in our last chapter, there is very little specific instruction in the Bible on the mechanics of **how** to pray, and this is understandable given that prayer is a matter of relationship with the true and living God, not a technique to be mastered and then utilised. However, the good news is that the Bible does offer us considerable advice in knowing **what** to pray. In fact, we might almost say that the **how** of prayer in the Bible is the same as the **what**. When teaching his disciples to pray, Jesus didn't give instruction on posture or style, or exercises to get in the mood; he taught the disciples six things to pray for: "hallowed be your name", "your kingdom come", "your will be done", and so on. (We'll come back to the prayer Jesus taught later in this chapter.)

In this chapter (and the next), we'll look at how the Bible teaches us what to pray for under two headings: 'The desires of God' and 'The anxieties of life'.

JESUS REMINDS US, "If you then, who are evil, know how to give good gifts to your children, how much more will your Father who is in heaven give good things to those who ask him!" (Matt 7:11).

As we've already seen, God is powerfully able and more than willing to shower us with good things. But **what are the good things he is ready to give us?** What blessings does God long to send down? What are his desires for us—his plans, wishes, priorities and aspirations for us? What does God want for us?

If we could find the answers to these questions, we could pray to God for these things with great confidence, knowing that God really wants to give them to us. This is the meaning of this wonderful but often-misunderstood verse in the Psalms:

> Delight yourself in the LORD,
>   and he will give you the desires of your heart.
> (Ps 37:4)

This verse is sometimes taken to mean that if we praise God (perhaps in song) and make him our number one priority in life, then God will give us all the things we really want—that special person to marry, that dream job, a happy family, and so on—as if God were saying, "You do the right thing by me, and I'll fulfil all your dreams".

But the message of the verse is quite different. If we delight ourselves in the LORD, what will that do to the desires of our hearts? If God is our joy and delight—if he matters more to us than anything in all the world—what effect will that have on the thoughts and dreams of our hearts? It will transform them. As we delight ourselves in the LORD, our thinking and wishes and aspirations will become like his. **We will want what God himself wants**. The desires of our hearts will become the desires of God and he will surely give them to us, as this verse so marvellously promises.

And so let us go to God and delight ourselves in him for a few pages, and have the desires of our hearts transformed. Let us dwell on what God really wants for us—what his plans are—what his desires are—and see how that might affect our prayers.

1. Delight yourself in his plans

God's desires are revealed for us in several ways in the Bible. Firstly, we can look at the plans of God. We can examine what his intentions and purposes are and thus see what it is that he most desires. In one sense, the whole Bible is the story of God's unfolding plan for humanity and his creation. From creation through redemption to new creation, God has a plan for the world he has made and that plan focuses on Jesus Christ.

There are numerous places where God's grand plan for his world and for us as individuals is summarized. None are more powerful, perhaps, than the first chapter of Paul's letter to the Ephesians:

> Blessed be the God and Father of our Lord Jesus
> Christ, who has blessed us in Christ with every
> spiritual blessing in the heavenly places, even as he
> chose us in him before the foundation of the world,
> that we should be holy and blameless before him. In
> love he predestined us for adoption through Jesus
> Christ, according to the purpose of his will, to the
> praise of his glorious grace, with which he has blessed
> us in the Beloved. In him we have redemption
> through his blood, the forgiveness of our trespasses,
> according to the riches of his grace, which he lavished
> upon us, in all wisdom and insight making known to
> us the mystery of his will, according to his purpose,
> which he set forth in Christ as a plan for the fullness
> of time, to unite all things in him, things in heaven
> and things on earth. (Eph 1:3-10)

From before the foundation of the world, God has been

working to save and redeem and adopt his own people from every nation—both Jew and Gentile—that they might be united together under one head: Jesus Christ. God's secret, history-wide plan, which has now finally been made known, is to "unite all things in [Christ], things in heaven and things on earth".

The same majestic plan of God is expressed time and again in different words in the New Testament. Take some time to dwell on the following passages and ask yourself, "What is God's desire for me? What is his plan, not just for the world in general, but for me?"

> And we know that for those who love God all things
> work together for good, for those who are called
> according to his purpose. For those whom he
> foreknew he also predestined to be conformed to
> the image of his Son, in order that he might be the
> firstborn among many brothers. And those whom
> he predestined he also called, and those whom he
> called he also justified, and those whom he justified
> he also glorified. (Rom 8:28-30)

> For the grace of God has appeared, bringing salvation
> for all people, training us to renounce ungodliness
> and worldly passions, and to live self-controlled,
> upright, and godly lives in the present age, waiting
> for our blessed hope, the appearing of the glory of
> our great God and Saviour Jesus Christ, who gave
> himself for us to redeem us from all lawlessness and
> to purify for himself a people for his own possession
> who are zealous for good works. (Tit 2:11-14)

> But we ought always to give thanks to God for you,
> brothers beloved by the Lord, because God chose
> you as the firstfruits to be saved, through
> sanctification by the Spirit and belief in the truth.
> To this he called you through our gospel, so that
> you may obtain the glory of our Lord Jesus Christ.
> So then, brothers, stand firm and hold to the
> traditions that you were taught by us, either by our
> spoken word or by our letter. (2 Thess 2:13-15)

> Finally, then, brothers, we ask and urge you in the
> Lord Jesus, that as you received from us how you
> ought to live and to please God, just as you are
> doing, that you do so more and more. For you know
> what instructions we gave you through the Lord
> Jesus. For this is the will of God, your sanctification
> ... (1 Thess 4:1-3)

What is God's desire for us? What is his purpose for each one of us? That we be conformed to the image of his Son; that we become part of a new people who are purified from their sin and zealous for good works; and that we stand firm and live in holiness, and finally obtain the glory of our Lord Jesus Christ.

The same truth can be repeated in lots of ways. This is what God wants for us and, in Christ, plans to give us. Is it what we want for ourselves?

The answer is very often 'No'. As Galatians 5 reminds us, the desires of God's Spirit within us are at war with the desires of our own flesh. By nature, we don't want what God wants. And this is why we need to pray that God would fulfil his plans and desires for us and within us—that his Spirit would produce in us the fruit of love, joy, peace, patience, kindness, goodness, faithfulness, gentleness and self-control (Gal 5:22-23). Note Paul's prayer for the Thessalonians:

> To this end we always pray for you, that our God may make you worthy of his calling and may fulfil every resolve for good and every work of faith by his power, so that the name of our Lord Jesus may be glorified in you, and you in him, according to the grace of our God and the Lord Jesus Christ.
> (2 Thess 1:11-12)

In knowing what God's intentions are—his plans for us in Christ—we are provided with rich content for our prayers. We can pray confidently with assurance for the things that God desires for us, knowing that he will grant our requests.

2. Delight yourself in his promises

God's desires are also revealed in his many promises. When God makes a promise in Scripture, it is an expression of what he wants to give us. More than that, it's an expression of what he guarantees he will give us.

Take a promise such as that contained in Acts 10:43: "To him all the prophets bear witness that everyone who believes in him receives forgiveness of sins through his name". Where God gives a clear promise like this, we can confidently call upon him to fulfil it because we know that he is faithful. We can confess our sins to him, knowing that he will hear us and faithfully keep his promise to forgive us.

Here is a very brief sample of scriptural promises that we can confidently call upon God to fulfil:

> If any of you lacks wisdom, let him ask God, who gives generously to all without reproach, and it will be given him. (Jas 1:5)

> No temptation has overtaken you that is not common to man. God is faithful, and he will not let you be tempted beyond your ability, but with the temptation he will also provide the way of escape, that you may be able to endure it. (1 Cor 10:13)

> If we confess our sins, he is faithful and just to forgive us our sins and to cleanse us from all unrighteousness. (1 John 1:9)

> He will wipe away every tear from their eyes, and death shall be no more, neither shall there be mourning nor crying nor pain anymore, for the former things have passed away. (Rev 21:4)

> No, in all these things we are more than conquerors through him who loved us. For I am sure that neither death nor life, nor angels nor rulers, nor things present nor things to come, nor powers, nor height nor depth, nor anything else in all creation, will be able to separate us from the love of God in Christ Jesus our Lord. (Rom 8:37-39)

Blessed are the pure in heart, for they shall see God. (Matt 5:8)

Draw near to God, and he will draw near to you. (Jas 4:8a)

Cast your burden on the LORD,
    and he will sustain you;
he will never permit
    the righteous to be moved. (Ps 55:22)

... as far as the east is from the west,
    so far does he remove our transgressions from
        us. (Ps 103:12)

These marvellous and sure promises from our Father can provide content to our prayers. However, to avoid any misunderstanding, we need to notice **when** God has promised to grant us these things. For example, the first three promises listed above—for wisdom, a way of escape from temptation, and forgiveness—are promises for **now**, and we can pray confidently, trusting that God will fulfil these promises in our present experience. However, the fourth promise listed from Revelation 21:4 is for the future glorious age of his kingdom when "the former things have passed away". We can and should still pray that God would bring this about but we need to recognize the difference in timing.

3. Delight yourself in his commands

We can also discern what God desires for us—and what we can therefore pray for with confidence—by looking at the commands of the Bible. If God commands us to do something—to love one another as Jesus loved us, for example—then we can be sure that this is one of his desires for us (i.e. that we be loving towards each other). And so this is something we can pray for ourselves and for others: "Lord, so work in me by your Spirit that I grow in love for others, laying down my life for them, as Jesus did for me".

The many commands of God in the Bible—from the Ten Commandments through to the instructions Paul gives in his letters in the New Testament—can thus supply a steady stream of God-centred requests for our prayers.

4. Delight yourself in the prayers of Scripture

Another obvious way to discover what God really desires for us is to look at all the examples of godly prayer that are provided for us in the Bible. As we read these inspired prayers, we catch a glimpse of what God really wants us to ask for as we approach him. We see modelled for us requests that are focused on God's desires for us.

To take but one example, look at Paul's marvellous prayer for the Colossians:

And so, from the day we heard, we have not ceased to pray for you, asking that you may be filled with the knowledge of his will in all spiritual wisdom and understanding, so as to walk in a manner worthy of the Lord, fully pleasing to him, bearing fruit in every good work and increasing in the knowledge of God. May you be strengthened with all power, according to his glorious might, for all endurance and patience with joy, giving thanks to the Father, who has qualified you to share in the inheritance of the saints in light. (Col 1:9-12)

How different our lives might be—and those of our friends and family and church—if this was our constant prayer! What greater need do we have than to be filled with the knowledge of his will, to walk in a manner worthy of him, to please him and bear fruit in every good work, and to be strengthened so that we might endure with patience and joy? And what greater desire does God have than to grant us all these things?

The prayers of the Bible offer us brilliant models of praying for the desires of God. For example, take a close look at:

- Paul's prayers in Philippians 1:9-11, 2 Thessalonians 1:11-12, and Ephesians 3:14-21;
- the prayers of Jesus in John 17 and Mark 14:34-36;
- the godly prayers of Daniel (Dan 9:1-19), Nehemiah (Neh 1:4-11) and the Levites (Neh 9:5-38);
- the majestic prayers of the Psalms (such as Ps 51 or Ps 39).

Of course, the supreme model of scriptural prayer is the one explicitly put forward by Jesus which we know as the Lord's Prayer (Matt 6:9-13; cf. Luke 11:2-4).

It is a wonderfully simple prayer and yet there is a world of biblical teaching about prayer contained in its few words.

Take the opening address to God: "Our Father in heaven". This expresses nearly everything we saw in chapters 2 and 3 about the nature of God and our relationship with him, which is the foundation of prayer. God is the loving, gracious **Father** who is willing to listen and to act, and upon whom we depend for everything. In addition, we are now related to him as adopted children through the work of Christ. He is **our** Father. And this gracious Father, to whom we relate as sons, is the powerful God of all the world—that is, he is enthroned **in heaven**.

The six requests that then make up the content of the prayer are all about the plans and desires of God—that is, they are focused on the kingdom of God which is coming in Christ. In particular, the prayer seems to reflect the expectations and promises of the prophecy of Ezekiel in chapters 36 and 37. The kingdom that we pray for in the Lord's prayer is the promised messianic kingdom of Ezekiel in which, out of concern for his holy name, God brings salvation and mercy and restoration to his people.

Let's look at each of the six requests briefly.

i. "hallowed be your name"

Three pieces of background information will help us understand this well-known opening request of the Lord's Prayer. The first is that the word 'hallow' simply means 'to make holy', and to make something 'holy' means to demonstrate how precious or special or distinctive it is. Secondly, in biblical times, a person's name stood for their reputation and character. So to make someone's name holy meant to establish in the eyes of all that this person was very special—to put them on a pedestal so that everyone would recognize how glorious and wonderful that person was. It was the opposite of ruining or besmirching someone's name.

This first request in the Lord's Prayer, therefore, is asking God to enhance his own reputation—to put his own name 'up in lights' so that everyone will recognize how wonderful and powerful and great he truly is. How would God do such a thing? The answer to that lies in the third piece of useful background information in Ezekiel 36. In this prophecy, God points out that Israel has defiled and blasphemed his name among the nations. They have made God's name mud—not only because of their wicked behaviour, but because of the punishment that this behaviour has brought upon them. God's wrath has been poured out on them "for the blood that they had shed in the land, for the idols with which they had defiled it" (v. 18). They have been defeated in battle and scattered among the nations round about (v. 19). And so the nations looking on have said, "These are the people of the LORD, and yet they had to go out of his land" (v. 20). The prophecy continues:

> "Therefore say to the house of Israel, Thus says the
> Lord GOD: It is not for your sake, O house of Israel,
> that I am about to act, but for the sake of my holy
> name, which you have profaned among the nations
> to which you came. And I will vindicate the holiness
> of my great name, which has been profaned among
> the nations, and which you have profaned among
> them. And the nations will know that I am the
> LORD, declares the Lord GOD, when through you I
> vindicate my holiness before their eyes. I will take
> you from the nations and gather you from all the
> countries and bring you into your own land. I will
> sprinkle clean water on you, and you shall be clean
> from all your uncleannesses, and from all your idols
> I will cleanse you." (Ezek 36:22-25)

God declares that he will act to rescue and redeem his scattered people and make them clean once more. And he will do so not because they deserve it, but "for the sake of my holy name".

To pray for God to 'hallow his name' is to pray for him to bring his promised salvation and kingdom. It is begging God to answer the scorn and mockery of the pagans by acting powerfully and mightily to save his people—not for their sake, but for the sake of his holy name.

We live in a world where God's name is still

mocked and derided—"There is no fear of God before their eyes" (Rom 3:18). In the first request of the Lord's Prayer, we plead with God to do something about this —to redeem his people, to bring in his kingdom so that the mouths of the mockers will be shut. It is a prayer, in other words, for world evangelization and the coming of God's kingdom.

Like Paul in Acts 17 when he observes the idolatry of Athens, we should burn with indignation that God's reputation lies in ruins in our world. And so we pray that he would do something about it—that his name would be honoured and 'hallowed' by all.

ii. "your kingdom come"

The second request follows directly on from the first. In fact, it means much the same thing. When God's kingdom comes, his name will be hallowed, and God will hallow his name by bringing in his kingdom.

Again, this is the message of Ezekiel. In chapter 37, Ezekiel prophesies of the time to come when God will restore the kingdom to Israel:

> "And I will make them one nation in the land, on
> the mountains of Israel. And one king shall be king
> over them all, and they shall be no longer two
> nations, and no longer divided into two kingdoms.
> They shall not defile themselves anymore with their
> idols and their detestable things, or with any of
> their transgressions. But I will save them from all

the backslidings in which they have sinned, and will cleanse them; and they shall be my people, and I will be their God.

"My servant David shall be king over them, and they shall all have one shepherd. They shall walk in my rules and be careful to obey my statutes. They shall dwell in the land that I gave to my servant Jacob, where your fathers lived. They and their children and their children's children shall dwell there forever, and David my servant shall be their prince forever." (Ezek 37:22-25)

When will this promised kingdom come? Earlier in Matthew's Gospel, both John the Baptist and Jesus have declared that the kingdom "is at hand" (3:2; 4:17). Later in the Gospel, Jesus tells the unbelieving Pharisees that his miraculous exorcisms indicate that "the kingdom of God has come upon you" (Matt 12:28). The perspective of the New Testament is that with the coming of Jesus, the Messianic Son of David and the Good Shepherd, the promised kingdom of God has dawned in our world. The sun has crested above the horizon and its spreading rays are bringing light to the world. Membership of the kingdom is now open to all by repenting and putting your trust in Jesus. And some of the benefits of the kingdom—such as forgiveness of sins and receiving God's Spirit—can now be enjoyed. Like a mustard seed that grows into a large, flourishing plant, the kingdom is growing throughout the world. But the full light of day is not yet here and it won't be here until Jesus comes again and God's universal kingdom is demonstrated to all.

This is what the second request of the Lord's Prayer is for. It's asking God to bring his kingdom—both in its spread throughout the world and in its final glory— when every knee will bow to Jesus as the king.

iii. "your will be done, on earth as it is in heaven"

The third request sounds like more of the same and, in one sense, it is. Wherever God is acknowledged as king, his will is done. And when the kingdom finally does come in its entirety, God's will—his plans, his wishes, his purposes for the world—will finally be accomplished here on earth, just as it is presently in heaven.

Once more, the background of Ezekiel 36-37 helps us to see a little more in this third request. In Ezekiel, God made it clear that judgement and destruction had fallen on Israel because of their gross disobedience and backsliding. Not only had they blasphemed God's name among the nations, they had also defiled the good land which God had given them:

> "Son of man, when the house of Israel lived in their own land, they defiled it by their ways and their deeds. Their ways before me were like the uncleanness of a woman in her menstrual impurity. So I poured out my wrath upon them for the blood that they had shed in the land, for the idols with which they had defiled it." (Ezek 36:17-18)

God's will was most definitely not being done in his land and so he banished his people from it.

The marvellous promise of Ezekiel's prophecy is that, when God finally acts to restore his people and return them to their land, their behaviour will be different:

> "And I will give you a new heart, and a new spirit I will put within you. And I will remove the heart of stone from your flesh and give you a heart of flesh. And I will put my Spirit within you, and cause you to walk in my statutes and be careful to obey my rules. You shall dwell in the land that I gave to your fathers, and you shall be my people, and I will be your God." (Ezek 36:26-28)

This time they will not defile the land by their disobedience. God's laws and statutes will be done in the land because his people will be empowered to do them by his own Spirit. They will "walk" in them day by day.

The third request of the Lord's Prayer reflects this promise. It claims the promise of Ezekiel that God will bring his reign into our very hearts, dwelling there by his Spirit and enabling us to walk in his ways. It asks that God would cause his will to be done here upon earth in the lives of his people, as it is in heaven.

THE SECOND SET OF THREE requests (requests four to six) shifts the focus more to us and our concerns. But it's a shift in emphasis or focus, not a change of subject. The kingdom of God is still the central content of these three requests. If the first three ask God to be God and to extend his saving kingdom into all the world, the second three ask that the blessings of this kingdom would come to **us**. They ask that we would experience the kingdom in our own lives and that we would be protected by God's power until the day when the kingdom comes in all its fullness.

iv. "give us today tomorrow's bread"*

The fourth request for 'bread' is phrased a little unusually. It asks for a particular kind of bread—our bread of 'tomorrow' or of 'the day to come'. (This is a better translation than the traditional 'daily bread'.) What sort of bread is this 'bread of tomorrow'? And why would we want to ask for it today?

The place to look for answers, as with the other requests in the Lord's Prayer, is in the patterns and promises of the Old Testament. From the time when Israel receives 'tomorrow's bread today' in the provision of manna in the wilderness (Exod 16), the theme of bread and God's provision pops up regularly in the history of Israel. The promised land itself was to be a place of abundance and rich food, a land flowing with milk and honey, with vineyards and olive orchards that they did not plant. It was a 'rest' (or 'Sabbath') where

---

*   Our translation; cf. ESV margin.

Israel could enjoy safety from her enemies and receive the rich blessings that God had promised them by his grace (e.g. Josh 24:13; 1 Kgs 4:24-25). When, in the course of time, Israel sinned and was judged by God, they lost this rich abundance. They suffered famine and, eventually, exile under God's judgement.

In Ezekiel 36 God promises to reverse this situation. Immediately after the passage that appears to lie behind the third request (Ezek 36:26-28) come these verses:

> "And I will deliver you from all your uncleannesses. And I will summon the grain and make it abundant and lay no famine upon you. I will make the fruit of the tree and the increase of the field abundant, that you may never again suffer the disgrace of famine among the nations." (Ezek 36:29-30)

In the coming kingdom, God is going to satisfy the hunger and poverty that his people have experienced. In the day to come—the day of the kingdom—they will experience his abundant blessing and never again suffer the indignity of famine. This image of the coming messianic kingdom as one in which there is abundant food and eating is found elsewhere in the Old Testament prophets (e.g. Isa 25:6-9; 65:13-14). It's an image picked up later in Matthew's Gospel as well, where Jesus describes the coming kingdom as a great feast (Matt 8:11; 22:1-14).

Could it be that to ask to be given today the 'bread

of tomorrow' is to ask for the blessings of the coming kingdom? Is it asking that we might receive the glories of the messianic feast to come? In light of the very strong focus of all the other requests on the coming kingdom of God, it seems likely that this is indeed what Jesus is saying.

This fourth request, then, is another request for the kingdom to come. It expresses a longing for the bread and abundance of the next age, rather than the uncertain and fading wealth of this age which is so prone to rust and decay and theft (as Jesus goes on to point out later in Matthew 6). These are the blessings that Jesus will bring when he returns in all his power, and we are to pray that his coming will be 'today'.

We can, of course, 'eat' of some of those blessings 'today' because Jesus has already come. The Bread of Life himself has come and died and risen and poured out his Spirit so that we might know now the joy of sins forgiven, of consciences cleansed and of God's love being poured into our hearts. We know peace with God and glad fellowship with his people. We will still suffer and groan now, as we wait for the final coming of the kingdom. But, through Christ, we are citizens of the kingdom of heaven now, as we seek and long for its coming.

v. "forgive us our debts"

Foremost among the blessings of the kingdom that the Old Testament prophets looked forward to was the forgiveness of sins. In our passage from Ezekiel, it's a promise repeated over and over again:

> "I will sprinkle clean water on you, and you shall be clean from all your uncleannesses, and from all your idols I will cleanse you." (Ezek 36:25)

> "And I will deliver you from all your uncleannesses." (Ezek 36:29a)

> "Thus says the Lord GOD: On the day that I cleanse you from all your iniquities, I will cause the cities to be inhabited, and the waste places shall be rebuilt." (Ezek 36:33)

> "They shall not defile themselves anymore with their idols and their detestable things, or with any of their transgressions. But I will save them from all the backslidings in which they have sinned, and will cleanse them; and they shall be my people, and I will be their God." (Ezek 37:23)

It is also the promise of Jeremiah's famous prophecy:

> "But this is the covenant that I will make with the house of Israel after those days, declares the LORD: I will put my law within them, and I will write it on their hearts. And I will be their God, and they shall be my people. And no longer shall each one teach his neighbour and each his brother, saying, 'Know the LORD,' for they shall all know me, from the least of them to the greatest, declares the LORD. For I will forgive their iniquity, and I will remember their sin no more." (Jer 31:33-34)

The fifth request of the Lord's Prayer asks that this benefit of the kingdom be given to us. It is an acknowledgement that we will continue to falter and fail and do the wrong thing as the kingdom approaches, and that we aren't fit to enter the kingdom of the righteous, holy God unless these sins are dealt with.

The simple heartfelt prayer of the tax collector in Luke 18:13—"God, be merciful to me, a sinner!"—remains the basic lifelong prayer of the Christian. The kingdom we long for is a kingdom of forgiveness. It's a kingdom of light, where evil deeds are exposed, acknowledged, seen for what they are and then forgiven through the atoning sacrifice of Christ on our behalf.

The sting in the tail of this request is that if we want to belong to this kingdom of forgiveness, then we'd better extend the same forgiveness to those who wrong us. It's not a claim for forgiveness on the basis of good works, as if the request was, "Forgive us our sins **because we deserve it**, since, after all, we forgive those who sin against us". But it is a very serious statement that we can't expect to belong to a kingdom of forgiveness if we don't believe in forgiveness! If, by our behaviour towards others, we declare, "I don't think people ought to be forgiven—they should receive all the punishment that they deserve", then we have ruled out the possibility of forgiveness for ourselves as well. (We'll come back to this idea in chapter 8.)

vi. "lead us not into testing but deliver us from the evil one"*

The three requests in the second half of the Lord's Prayer focus on life in this world as we wait and long for the coming kingdom. Given that we look forward to the promised kingdom and recognize that it has already dawned in Jesus, we ask to eat of its bread today, to receive forgiveness so that we may enter it, and (in this final request) to be preserved in the midst of this present evil age. The world in which we live as we wait for the coming kingdom remains the world of testing and difficulty. Our adversary the devil still prowls like a roaring lion, seeking someone to devour (1 Pet 5:8). The opposition, persecution and hatred that Jesus suffered will also be the lot of his disciples (John 15:18-20).

The final double-barrelled request of the Lord's Prayer recognizes that, as the kingdom approaches, life will not be easy for those who long for it and belong to it by faith. We desperately want to survive as Christians and to wait faithfully for the revealing of God's kingdom, but we know only too well that we are frail and weak and prone to giving up. This final request acknowledges our ongoing dependence on God—that he would shelter us from the testings that might bring us down, and deliver us from the evil one who at times seems so strong as to overpower us.

---

* Our translation.

THE LORD'S PRAYER IS A marvellous template for our requests to God. It homes in on God's desires—on what is important to him and therefore what should be important to us. It focuses on his plans—on the coming kingdom of Jesus the Messiah. It teaches us that God desires and plans:

- for his name to be revered and honoured as the mighty Saviour;
- for his kingdom to come in all its fullness;
- for his kingdom to extend here and now throughout the world in the lives of people as they submit to his rule;
- for his people to taste the blessings of that kingdom now;
- to forgive our sins and for us to live by forgiveness;
- to deliver us from the evil one and his testings.

As with all of the other desires of God we have looked at in this chapter, we can confidently bring these requests to our heavenly Father, knowing that he will grant them.

This leaves us with a question, of course. What about all those matters about which God is silent—matters where we do not know what God wants or desires to give us? How do we know what to pray for in those circumstances?

That's the subject of our next chapter.

In the meantime, think about how you can shape your prayers according to the desires of God. Some

Christians do this by keeping a 'prayer notebook' in which they jot down scriptural promises, examples and subjects for prayer. Then they use this list each day in their prayers for particular people. Why not start your own list of the 'desires of God', using the examples in this chapter, and then add to it as you read the Scriptures.

Chapter 7

THE ANXIETIES OF LIFE

IF WE WANT TO KNOW WHAT to pray for, the starting place should be what God wants for us. In the previous chapter, we looked at how God's desires should dominate our prayers and how we can find out what those desires are from the Bible.

However, where does that leave the multitude of daily hassles, problems and issues that we are concerned about and which we want to bring to God in prayer? Is it somehow wrong, or perhaps less worthy, to bother God with these things? We may be able to pray confidently for God's own desires for us, but does that mean that we can have no confidence in bringing other requests to God?

Imagine, for example, that your son has a speech

impediment and is being picked on at school. You are distressed and worried about how he will cope, about how it will affect his overall attitude to school, and about what long-term psychological effects the bullying might have.

What do you pray for? Obviously you pray for the speech impediment to be cured and the bullying to stop. But do we have any assurance that either of these things are God's will for your son at this time? There is no scriptural promise that Christians will be spared medical or other problems in life, such as speech impediments. Nor does God say that he will always prevent people being mean to other people.

What, then, do we pray? And what confidence can we have in God's answer?

The Bible says nothing about the specifics of what to pray for in this and a thousand other similar, daily situations, but it is not at all silent about what we should do with the anxieties of life. We should bring them to God.

1. No anxiety about anything

The Bible quite explicitly urges us to bring the anxieties of life to God. As Paul says to his friends in Philippi,

> ... do not be anxious about anything, but in
> everything by prayer and supplication with

thanksgiving let your requests be made known to
God. (Phil 4:6)

This could hardly be more all-inclusive or more
comforting. Is any anxiety too great or too small to
bring to God in prayer? Paul is very clear about it: do
not be anxious about **anything**, but in **everything** let
your requests be made known to God.

Are you worried or anxious about your kids? About
your job, your finances, your health, your church, your
neighbours, your spouse, your friends, your family,
your future, your soul? What is it that leaves you
fearful? What is the nagging worry that distracts your
attention and disturbs your sleep? **Whatever** it is, Paul
encourages us to talk to God about it.

He can say this because he is confident, as he says
later in Philippians, that "my God will supply every
need of yours according to his riches in glory in Christ
Jesus" (Phil 4:19). Nothing is too big for God to handle
and nothing is too small for his attention. He is very
capable of sustaining us and providing for us. So why
worry? Jesus makes exactly this point in the famous
passage from the Sermon on the Mount:

> "Therefore I tell you, do not be anxious about your
> life, what you will eat or what you will drink, nor
> about your body, what you will put on. Is not life
> more than food, and the body more than clothing?
> Look at the birds of the air: they neither sow nor

reap nor gather into barns, and yet your heavenly
Father feeds them. Are you not of more value than
they? And which of you by being anxious can add
a single hour to his span of life? And why are you
anxious about clothing? Consider the lilies of the
field, how they grow: they neither toil nor spin, yet
I tell you, even Solomon in all his glory was not
arrayed like one of these. But if God so clothes the
grass of the field, which today is alive and tomorrow
is thrown into the oven, will he not much more
clothe you, O you of little faith? Therefore do not be
anxious, saying, 'What shall we eat?' or 'What shall
we drink?' or 'What shall we wear?' For the Gentiles
seek after all these things, and your heavenly Father
knows that you need them all. But seek first the
kingdom of God and his righteousness, and all these
things will be added to you.

Therefore do not be anxious about tomorrow, for
tomorrow will be anxious for itself. Sufficient for
the day is its own trouble." (Matt 6:25-34)

Prayer in the midst of anxiety is such an expression of
trust. It takes God at his word. I may be feeling anxious
or worried about any number of things, but I hear
God's word promising me that he knows what I need
and will supply it without fail. And so I put my trust in
his promise and call upon him to fulfil it.

2. A Christian mind

When we are faced by the anxieties of life, what we pray for will be driven by what we believe. If we believe, as some do, that God's will is for Christians to be financially prosperous, then we will pray about our money worries in a certain way—for example, "Lord, I know that this current shortfall in my finances is not your will for me, and I pray that you would bless my finances and make me wealthy again". However, if we believe that poverty is actually a Christian virtue, as others in history have done, then we would pray very differently—for example, "Lord, thank you that you have blessed me with the same sort of poverty that Jesus had. I pray that you would help me to continue to trust you to provide all my needs." Our mind-set will determine the content of our prayers.

Becoming a Christian, of course, involves a decisive **change** of mind:

> Do not be conformed to this world, but be
> transformed by the **renewal of your mind**, that by
> testing you may discern what is the will of God,
> what is good and acceptable and perfect. (Rom 12:2)

How we think about our worries and anxieties, and therefore what we pray for in the midst of them, will be determined by our Christian mind. That mind is constantly being renewed and changed by the work of God in our lives. As his word penetrates and renovates our attitudes, assumptions and beliefs, it will change the way we pray. In the matter of our finances, a Christian mind will remember the prayer of Agur in Proverbs and pray accordingly.

> Remove far from me falsehood and lying;
>> give me neither poverty nor riches;
>> feed me with the food that is needful for me,
> lest I be full and deny you
>> and say, "Who is the LORD?"
> or lest I be poor and steal
>> and profane the name of my God. (Prov 30:8-9)

Or, to return to the example of our speech-impaired son being bullied at school, a transformed mind will not only pray the natural and perfectly reasonable prayer that the impediment be cured and that the bullying stop, it will also pray that the experience will strengthen our son's character and trust in God, according to the biblical assumption that faith and trust in God, and resilience of character, are produced in the furnace of difficulty and suffering. In love we may also pray for the bully—that his mind and heart would be changed: "Love your enemies and pray for those who persecute you" (Matt 5:44).

The more our hearts and minds are changed by the work of God's Word and Spirit, the more our prayers will reflect God's own mind. However, our minds will not be fully renewed and perfected this side of glory, and we will never know fully what God wants for us, nor what we should pray for in every situation. And this is why the prayer of the Christian amidst the anxieties of life will always echo the prayer of Jesus to his Father in Gethsemane: "Nevertheless, not my will, but yours, be done" (Luke 22:42).

Strangely, some people are critical of this prayer. Christians should not pray this, they say, because it exhibits a lack of faith. Christians should 'name it and claim it' and not waste their breath on these sorts of namby-pamby, cop-out-style prayers. Know what you want to ask from God and claim it in faith—and if you believe it strongly enough, you'll get it. This view is mistaken because it confuses the 'desires of God' with the 'anxieties of life'.

When we know what God's will is, we can and should pray confidently. Faith demands that we do. This is what we saw in our last chapter. If God **has** revealed his will about something—for example, that we should not steal—then it's pointless, not to say grossly disobedient, to pray, "Lord, I'm not sure whether you want me to steal. You know how poor I am. You know how having more money would make such a difference to our lives and how the taxation system is so unjust. So I commit this to you and ask that you give me a peace about what I should do. Thy will be done!"

However, God's purposes aren't always as clear as "You shall not steal". Amidst the hassles and problems and anxieties of life, the prayer of faith is the one which pours out its anxiety and entrusts the outcome to God's good and sovereign will.

3. With thanksgiving

When Paul urges the Philippians to bring all the anxieties of life to God, he adds two very important words:

> ... do not be anxious about anything, but in everything
> by prayer and supplication **with thanksgiving** let
> your requests be made known to God. (Phil 4:6)

If we are going to express our trust in God by pouring all our fears and worries before him, that same trust will also result in thanksgiving for what he has already done for us.

We may be anxious, for example, about whether we are going to keep our job, and we will bring it before the Lord. But at the same time, we should also pour out our thanks to him that we ever had the job in the first place. We should thank him that we have worked in it and prospered over the past five years; that he has always provided us with food, clothing and shelter in abundance; that we live in a country where the opportunities for employment are numerous should this job fail; and so on. For every individual anxiety we may have, there are ten causes for thanksgiving. We should not forget this.

When we surround our requests to God with thanksgiving, we do the right thing on two counts. We rightly honour God and we wisely help ourselves.

Firstly, thanksgiving gives great glory and honour to God because it proclaims how good and merciful and generous he is towards us. We know that he is willing and able to answer our prayers, and we know that, incredibly, he allows us access to his very throne room. As Martin Luther says, "O how great a thing, how marvellous, a godly Christian's prayer is! How powerful with God; that a poor human creature should speak with God's high Majesty in heaven, and not be affrighted, but, on the contrary, **know that God smiles upon him for Christ's sake,** his dearly beloved Son."[1] As we come before God—even in our anxiety and sorrow—and see that he smiles on us because of Christ, how can we not thank him for allowing us into his presence? How can we not give him all the glory and praise and honour that is his due? As we do so— as we pour out our thanks for his innumerable blessings to us—we honour and glorify him. We treat him as the high, holy and wonderful God that he is.

Giving thanks to God for all his many benefits and gifts saves us from coming to him like an ungrateful, petulant child, demanding he fix our latest problem without any recognition that all we have has come from his hand.

Secondly, when we accompany our requests with thanksgiving, we also help ourselves. We lift our own spirits and change our perspective. Even as we speak and thank God for all his goodness to us, our worries

---

[1]   From *The Table Talk of Martin Luther*, Christian Focus, Fearn, 2003, p. 243.

and sorrows start to shrink in our minds. We recall the many ways in which God's goodness and kindness has been showered upon us in the past. We start to realize that the tally in our 'blessings' column makes the 'problems and anxieties' column look puny and almost insignificant. We may not immediately cease to worry or to grieve, but the whole tone of our prayer changes. Despair and self-pity start to evaporate and, in the midst of our anxiety, we remind ourselves of the ocean of blessing that our gracious God has already showered upon us.

In the midst of anxiety, we should always pray **with thanksgiving**.

4. God knows

One final thing to remember when we're praying about life's sufferings and anxieties is that, even when we aren't sure what to pray for, God himself knows what to pray for. In fact, his own Spirit, which he has given us, intercedes and prays for us according to his own will. This is the extraordinary reassurance we receive in Romans 8:

> Likewise the Spirit helps us in our weakness. For
> we do not know what to pray for as we ought, but
> the Spirit himself intercedes for us with groanings
> too deep for words. And he who searches hearts

knows what is the mind of the Spirit, because the
Spirit intercedes for the saints according to the will
of God. (Rom 8:26-27)

This is a rather profound passage and we do not have
time to explore all its depths. The main point, however,
is clear enough. Given the state of our world and the
state of our own weakness, we "do not know what to
pray for as we ought". But just as Jesus promised, God
does not leave us as orphans in the midst of our struggles in this "present evil age" (Gal 1:4). He himself
comes to us in the person of his Spirit and dwells within
us. And the Spirit, who is our helper and advocate, prays
to God on our behalf. It is not a spoken prayer—we do
not hear the words, and who knows if words are even
used—but, because God knows the mind of the Spirit,
and indeed because the Spirit knows what God's will is,
he can pray rightly on our behalf. We might not know
what to pray for but the Spirit does.

If it sounds surprising or strange to say that the
Spirit prays to God on our behalf, we should
remember that God the Son also prayed to God during
his time on earth. Indeed, as Paul points out later in
Romans 8, he still intercedes for us at the right hand
of God (Rom 8:34). Through his Spirit coming to live
within us, God so joins himself to us—so identifies
himself with our weakness and our groaning—that he
intercedes for us. We might well echo Paul's words
from the end of Romans 11:

Oh, the depth of the riches and wisdom and
knowledge of God! How unsearchable are his
judgements and how inscrutable his ways!

> "For who has known the mind of the Lord,
>   or who has been his counselor?"
> "Or who has given a gift to him
>   that he might be repaid?"

For from him and through him and to him are all
things. To him be glory forever. Amen. (vv. 33-36)

We cannot know everything that God has in store for
us. We cannot begin to fathom the riches and wisdom
and judgements and inscrutable ways of God. What
we can know—with complete certainty and assurance
—is that he is the Lord, the mighty and sovereign one,
who will work everything out according to his good
purposes. In the midst of all our anxieties we can trust
him completely.

Chapter 8

WHAT HAPPENS
WHEN WE PRAY?

As you pray, do you ever experience that nagging
sense that it's really a waste of time?

I can believe that God is there, and that he sent his
Son into the world. I can believe that through his
redeeming work I can have access to the Father in
prayer. I can even believe that the God who is the
supreme Lord of all, and who is 'all in all', can hear me
and relate to me individually.

But when I utter my meagre little string of words,
sitting in my bedroom, does he really **hear** me? Does
he listen to my words and respond to them? Does what
I have to say really have an impact on the mind and will
of the Creator and Lord of the Universe? If he is the
sovereign Lord whose plans can never be thwarted,

what reasonable hope can I have that my puny requests will make the slightest difference to his divine will? Does anything actually change when I pray?

Sometimes it doesn't seem to. Things just go on as they were, for better or worse. I pray and pray for sick relatives, but their condition worsens. Or I pray for my sick child and keep administering the antibiotics, sensing in my heart of hearts that it's the antibiotics that are doing the job, not my prayers.

And even when some difficult situation, about which I have prayed, does improve, was it going to improve anyway? Did my prayer have anything to do with it?

All these thoughts go through most Christians' minds at some time or another. We wonder what **happens** when we pray. And when the thought, "Well, probably nothing really", enters our minds, the spirit of prayer withers and dies within us like a plant without roots.

In this chapter, we're going to confront these basic and quite crucial questions under two headings:

- Are our prayers heard?
- Do our prayers change anything?

1. Are our prayers heard?

This question can mean two things. We may be asking the simple question, "Does God actually listen and hear me when I talk to him?" Do my words get through to him in some way? Does the content of my request register with him?

If God is the almighty universal God of all, as the Scriptures reveal him to be, then this first aspect of the question is not difficult to answer. Of course God hears us. If he is aware of the tiniest sparrow as it falls to the ground, and if we are worth more than many sparrows (as Jesus says in Matt 10:29-31), then of course he is fully aware of what we say to him. He hears and understands all.

Then again, we may be asking the slightly more difficult question which relates to the other meaning of the word 'heard': "Does God **hearken** to my prayers?" Does he **heed** them and will he do what I ask? Does God always 'hear' me in the sense of responding to and granting my requests?

To answer this, we need to remember the distinction we drew in the last two chapters between the **desires of God** and **the anxieties of life.** When we pray for the desires of God—for those things which are close to God's own heart, as it were—we can be assured that he will grant our request. If we ask for anything that God has promised, which he has revealed as his will and intention for us, then we can know that not only has he heard the content of our request, but that he has 'heard' us in the other sense as well. He will remember his promise and act.

For example, God clearly promises forgiveness to those who call upon him for mercy. He promises wisdom from above for those who ask for it. He longs to see the character of his Son formed in us, as we grow in the fruit of the Spirit. His plan is for the glory of his Son to be displayed throughout all the world. These things (and the many others we looked at in chapter 6) are matters about which we can pray with complete confidence. As the Apostle John says:

> And this is the confidence that we have toward him, that if we ask anything according to his will he hears us. And if we know that he hears us in whatever we ask, we know that we have the requests that we have asked of him. (1 John 5:14-15)

When it comes to the **anxieties of life**, we also can have every confidence that God will listen to our requests, and guard us and keep us in Christ Jesus:

> ... do not be anxious about anything, but in everything by prayer and supplication with thanksgiving let your requests be made known to God. **And the peace of God, which surpasses all understanding, will guard your hearts and your minds in Christ Jesus**. (Phil 4:6-7)

The "peace of God" mentioned in this verse is not really a feeling of tranquillity or calm, although it may well lead to that. This "peace of God" is not a temporary halt in the troubles and anxieties of life, such as when we manage to snatch a little 'peace and quiet' in the middle of a busy week. God's peace is the profound security, rest and wellbeing that results from

God's victory over all trouble, strife and evil through the cross of Christ. By the victory of Jesus Christ at Calvary, God has defeated all our enemies and secured a lasting peace for us that can never be shaken. As Paul says elsewhere, there is nothing in all of creation—not even death itself—that can separate us from the love of God in Christ Jesus (Rom 8:38-39; this is also Paul's point in Philippians 4). In the midst of our anxieties, we can bring our troubles and worries to God, knowing that in everything the peace that he has won will guard us and keep us in Christ Jesus.

However, when we pour out our anxieties before the Father, we have no word or assurance from him that **his** solution to our anxiety will be the same as **our** proposed solution. God will only ever do what is best for us, but in the midst of the difficulties and problems of life, **he** is the one (not us) who will know what is best. Sometimes our instinctive or heartfelt request will not be in our own interests and so God will, in love, give us something different.

In many families, the children know that if they want to eat whatever they like, they ask Dad. "Dad, is it okay if I make myself a chocolate milkshake and follow it up with a triple-choc fudge biscuit, a chocolate bar and a packet of chips?" Dad looks up distractedly from whatever he's doing and says, "Hmm? Yeah, whatever."

Mum, however, who really cares about what her children eat, will think for a moment about what else has already been eaten today and reply, "No, I think you'd better have some fruit. And after that, if you're still hungry, you can have the milkshake and the biscuit, but forget the rest!"

The kids groan but there's no doubt which parent has been the more loving and caring, and which one has answered their 'prayer' in the best way—even if the six-year-old making the request doesn't understand or appreciate the reasons why.

Sometimes the things we call upon God to give us are about as helpful and healthy for us as the sugar-laden, chocoholic requests of our kids. And very often we don't understand why that thing which we desire so intently and which to us seems to be the solution to our anxieties is not in fact the best thing for us at all. God, who sees and knows all and who is wise beyond our understanding, knows what we need and he graciously gives it to us.

This is all very easy to acknowledge in theory or when not much is at stake. But when your tears are dripping like blood over a sick child, or you have a spouse with mental illness, or your rebellious teenager seems bent on self-destruction, it can be very hard to trust God's timing and God's answer. He may grant us the healing that we long for, but not immediately. Or his answer may be 'No', as it was for the Apostle Paul:

> So to keep me from being too elated by the
> surpassing greatness of the revelations, a thorn was
> given me in the flesh, a messenger of Satan to

harass me, to keep me from being too elated. Three times I pleaded with the Lord about this, that it should leave me. But he said to me, "My grace is sufficient for you, for my power is made perfect in weakness". Therefore I will boast all the more gladly of my weaknesses, so that the power of Christ may rest upon me. (2 Cor 12:7-9)

Paul desperately wanted his 'thorn' removed. Three times he pleaded with the Lord to take it from him. But God knew what Paul needed most: to learn about grace and how God's power is perfected in weakness. And so God's answer to Paul's heartfelt plea for relief was 'No', just as it was for the Lord Jesus when he asked to have the 'cup' taken away from him in Gethsemane.

God always hears us but his answer is not always 'Yes'.

Two provisos

God promises that his door is always open to listen to our prayers, but with two important provisos.

Firstly, when we come to God in prayer, it must be **in the name of the Lord Jesus Christ**. We cannot come to him in our own name. We cannot come to him because we've gone to church for years, or because we think we're quite good people (at least compared with our neighbours), or for any other reason. It's the death of Jesus for the forgiveness of our sins which opens the door and gives us free and open access to God's throne.

Secondly, and following on from this, we can only approach God in the name of Jesus **if we have dealt with sin**. Indeed, that's what coming to God in Jesus' name really means: it means repenting of the sin which keeps entangling us, confessing our failings and wrongdoings, and trusting in Jesus and his work on the cross to wash us clean and make us blameless and acceptable in the sight of the Father. It's impossible to come to God, brandishing the saving name of Jesus Christ to gain access, and yet be unrepentant of our sins. If there is sin in my heart—sin which I am fond of, and attached to, and will not relinquish—then I cannot come to God and expect that he will listen to me. Psalm 66:18 warns us of this:

> If I had cherished iniquity in my heart,
>   the Lord would not have listened.

This idea crops up surprisingly often in the Bible. Jesus warns us in the Sermon on the Mount that,

> ... if you forgive others their trespasses, your heavenly Father will also forgive you, but if you do not forgive others their trespasses, neither will your Father forgive your trespasses. (Matt 6:14-15)

James is also scathing about the person who approaches God in prayer but does not really trust God:

> For that person must not suppose that he will receive anything from the Lord; he is a double-minded man, unstable in all his ways. (Jas 1:7-8)

And later in his letter, James reinforces the point in even stronger terms:

> You do not have, because you do not ask. You ask and do not receive, because you ask wrongly, to spend it on your passions. You adulterous people! Do you not know that friendship with the world is enmity with God? Therefore whoever wishes to be a friend of the world makes himself an enemy of God. (Jas 4:2b-4)

All this should be a warning to us not to presume on our heavenly Father—not to treat him like a 'blessing machine'. As we've already seen, prayer is an expression of our **relationship** with God through the Lord Jesus Christ. If we are spurning that relationship by 'cherishing iniquity' in our hearts or by adulterously pursuing "friendship with the world", we cannot waltz into God's presence as if nothing is the matter and ask him to grant our requests.

Let us not misunderstand this point or turn it into something it is not. Some people teach that if God doesn't grant our requests it is because of unconfessed sin in our life. And if we reply that we aren't aware of any unconfessed sin, we are told that there must be some sin there somewhere, buried in our past, which needs to be confessed. The idea is that, if we succeed in remembering and confessing every individual wrong act we have ever perpetrated, then and only then will the floodgates of God's blessing be poured out upon us.

This is hardly what the above passages are talking about. They describe a heart that cherishes sin—a heart that is cold towards others and has no interest in forgiveness—a heart that is now more comfortable in the friendship of the world than in the friendship of God. They describe a rebellious and wavering Christian who wants to have a foot in both camps—who is double-minded and who sees God as a means for enriching himself to make his life more enjoyable. This person, says James, should not expect to receive anything from the Lord.

How different is the person described by Psalm 37 (the passage we looked at earlier in chapter 6):

> Delight yourself in the LORD,
> and he will give you the desires of your heart.
> (Ps 37:4)

Those who delight themselves in the LORD will long for what the LORD longs for. Their hearts will desire the desires of God, and God will most certainly grant those desires.

2. Do our prayers change anything?

There are times when Christians doubt whether God is listening, or whether he is powerful enough to act and make a difference in this world. But there are other times when we worry that God is too powerful.

If he is indeed the almighty sovereign Lord of all, then what difference can my pathetic little prayers make? Should I expect that the awesome Majesty on high will drop everything and alter his plans because a man of dust happens to mumble some words in his direction? Can we really expect that our prayers change anything?

a. The simple answer

The simple answer to this question must be, "Yes, our prayers do make a difference because the Bible says that they do". In a passage we have already quoted, James says,

> You do not have, because you do not ask. You ask
> and do not receive, because you ask wrongly, to
> spend it on your passions. (Jas 4:2b-3).

"You do not have, because you do not ask." This could hardly be clearer. If they had asked, they would have received. But they didn't ask, so they didn't receive. Their asking was the thing that made the difference.

This is the extraordinary promise of God—that he changes things in response to our prayers. Of course, he doesn't give us **everything** that we ask for, as James also points out. If we ask and do not receive, it may well be because we are asking wrongly out of our self-ishness and love for this world.

However, the promise still stands. And to underline it, James highlights a striking biblical example:

> The prayer of a righteous person has great power as
> it is working. Elijah was a man with a nature like
> ours, and he prayed fervently that it might not rain,
> and for three years and six months it did not rain
> on the earth. Then he prayed again, and heaven
> gave rain, and the earth bore its fruit. (Jas 5:16b-18)

Elijah was a not a super-Christian or an angelic being. He was "a man with a nature like ours", says James. Yet when he prayed, it did not rain for three years. When he prayed again, it did rain. And this was not the only time Elijah achieved extraordinary results in prayer. While he was staying with the widow of Zarephath, the widow's only son died:

> And [Elijah] said to her, "Give me your son."
> And he took him from her arms and carried him up
> into the upper chamber where he lodged, and laid
> him on his own bed. And he cried to the LORD,
> "O LORD my God, have you brought calamity even
> upon the widow with whom I sojourn, by killing
> her son?" Then he stretched himself upon the child
> three times and cried to the LORD, "O LORD my
> God, let this child's life come into him again." And
> the LORD listened to the voice of Elijah. And the life
> of the child came into him again, and he revived.
> (1 Kings 17:19-22)

"And the LORD listened to the voice of Elijah." What a stunning sentence of Scripture that is! Who could. imagine that the mighty Lord of all would listen to the voice of a man? And yet that is what happened.

In answering our prayers, God brings change to our lives and circumstances. He responds to our requests. Our prayers really do make a difference.

b. Two errors

There is more to be said about how our prayers change things and, in particular, how our prayers relate to the sovereign will of God. But before we proceed, it is worth pausing to consider two ways in which Christians sometimes get this wrong.

We met the first error in chapter 4. It's the denial that prayer really does effect any change in the world—a denial made by such authors as William Barclay. In Barclay's view of prayer, God does not and cannot interfere with the natural course of events in our world, and so the only thing that prayer really changes is **us**. Through prayer we are strengthened and comforted in our struggles, but that is all. Prayer may change the life of the person who prays, but it does not bring about a change in the natural, orderly events of the world that God has set in motion.

Fortunately, nobody told Elijah about this when he was confronted with the lifeless body of the widow's son. And it seems that Isaiah had also not read Professor Barclay's books when he called upon the Lord to make the shadow retreat up the steps of Ahaz as a sign to King Hezekiah. And retreat it did (2 Kings 20).

Time and again in the Bible, ordinary people—people just like us, as James would say—pray for God to change the normal course of events in the world, and God hears and responds.

Even if we do not out-and-out deny that God responds to our prayers and acts within his world to change lives, circumstances and events, we may still deny it by our actions—that is, by our lack of prayer. In our heart of hearts, we trust in technology, science and human ingenuity to solve our problems, and we don't set much store in God intervening to change the situation. We half-heartedly pray for a relative to be healed of cancer, but we have no real expectation that God might do it. We send up a lame request or two for our boss to stop persecuting us, but we don't really have any hope that his hard-hearted, pig-headed, aggressive behaviour might change. In theory, we may believe that God is powerful to work in this world, and that he hears and responds to our prayers, but our lack of earnest prayer demonstrates that this belief has not penetrated our heart. We must repent of this and show our repentance by renewed prayer.

However, it is also possible to make the opposite error—to give our prayers too much power. Some people teach that God waits in heaven, ready to act, and that Christians have the power and authority to call forth his action. It only remains for them to pray—to 'name it and claim it'—and God will be bound to act. Notice how this view is reflected in the following quote:

The Soldier of the Cross had taught His disciples the need to pray, "Thy will be done on earth as it is in heaven". The obvious [implication] is that God has limited certain of His activities to responding to the prayers of His people. Unless they pray, He will not act. Heaven may will something to happen, but heaven waits and encourages earth's initiative to desire that will and then pray that it happens. The will of God is not done on earth by an inexorable, juggernaut omnipotence 'out there' overriding or ignoring the will of people on earth. On the contrary, God has willed that His hand be held back while He seeks for a person, an intercessor, to plead 'Thy will be done on earth', in this or that specific situation ... [1]

A popular mythology of 'intercession' has grown around this idea: if we only had the boldness to claim our authority—to bind and loose the powers of evil, to break down the demonic strongholds—then God's blessing would be released on our churches and societies. Ezekiel 22:30 is often quoted in support: "And I sought for a man among them who should build up the wall and stand in the breach before me for the land, that I should not destroy it, but I found none". This is the so-called role of the 'intercessor', to stand in the breach before God and make a difference.

---

[1]   R. A. Matthews, *Born for Battle*, OMF Books, Robesonia, 1978, p. 14; cited in Cindy Jacobs, *Possessing the Gates of the Enemy*, Chosen Books, Grand Rapids, 1991.

Frank Peretti's mega-best-selling novel, *This Present Darkness*, offers a powerful presentation of this view of prayer. The spiritual worldview of the novel is that an unseen but deadly battle is taking place all around us between demonic hordes of darkness and God's angels. And Christians participate in the battle through their prayers. When they pray, the angels gain new strength and the demons are beaten back; when they give up prayer, the demons overpower the angels and evil makes its way in the world. In one of the novel's climactic scenes, the evil Prince of Babylon, Rafar, is battling with an angel named Tal:

> Edith started to weep. "There's an evil spirit out there," she cried. "He's doing great mischief. His name is ... Raphael ... Raving ..."
>
> Bobby Corsi spoke up. "Rafar!"
>
> Edith looked at him with wide eyes. "Yes! Yes! That's the name the Lord's impressing upon me!"
>
> Tal could only back away from the fearsome onslaught of the demon prince, his one good hand still holding his sword up for defense. Rafar kept swinging and slashing, the sparks flying from the blades as they met. Tal's arm sank lower with each blow.
>
> "The Lord ... rebuke you!" Tal found the breath to say again.
>
> Edith Duster was on her feet and ready to shout it to the heavens. "Rafar, you wicked prince of evil, in the name of Jesus we rebuke you!"

Rafar's blade zinged over Tal's head. It missed.

"We bind you!" shouted the Remnant.

The big yellow eyes winced.

"We cast you out!" Andy asked.

There was a puff of sulfur, and Rafar bent over.
Tal leaped to his feet.

"We rebuke you, Rafar!" Edith shouted again.

Rafar screamed. Tal's blade had torn him open.

The big red blade came down with a clang against
Tal's, but that angelic sword was singing with a new
resonance. It cut through the air in fiery arcs. With his
one good hand, Tal kept swinging, slashing, cutting,
pushing Rafar back. The fiery eyes were oozing, the
foam was bubbling out the mouth and fizzing down
the chest, the yellow breath had turned deep crimson ...

The dripping, foaming jaws trembled open and the
words gargled through the tar and the froth. "But ...
for ... your ... praying saints! But for your saints ...!"

The big beast swayed forward. He let out one
last hissing sigh, and rumbled to the floor in a cloud
of red.

And it was quiet.[2]

---

2   F. E. Peretti, *This Present Darkness*, Crossway, Wheaton, 1986,
pp. 370-372.

This is fiction, of course. But it's how many people have come to think about prayer—as a kind of cosmic battleground in which the prayers of the saints are what make the difference between victory and defeat for God's kingdom.

If Professor Barclay's error robs prayer of its power, then this opposite and increasingly common error robs God of his sovereignty and gives human prayer too much prominence and power. God does not sit in heaven with his hands tied, waiting and hoping that someone will pray so that he can fulfil his plans. He is not dependent on our will and action, as if the progress of his work in the world hinges on whether we get out of bed and pray or not. His angels do not battle feebly against bigger, stronger demonic hordes, and it is not our prayers that win the victory over Satan. That victory has already been won through the death of the Lord Jesus, by which God "disarmed the rulers and authorities and put them to open shame, by triumphing over them in him" (Col 2:15).

Both of these errors are harmful. Both are to be resisted because they damage our prayer lives. The first error saps us of confidence and turns prayer into a form of self-improvement; the second gives us unrealistic expectations and turns prayer into a form of magic, which puts the divine power into human hands, to be called upon as we will (if the right formula and technique is used).

c. The more profound answer

What is the answer, then? How does the important biblical truth of God's sovereignty mesh together with the equally important biblical truth that our prayers do change things?

One of the best places to look for an answer is in the final chapters of the book of Job. It's hard to think of anywhere in the Bible that more powerfully portrays the absolute sovereignty, majesty and might of God than Job 38-41. After all his questioning and groaning to God about his suffering, in chapter 38 Job is confronted by God himself who has some questions of his own for Job to answer:

> Then the LORD answered Job out of the whirlwind and said:
>
> > "Who is this that darkens counsel by words
> > > without knowledge?
> > Dress for action like a man;
> > > I will question you, and you make it known to me.
> >
> > "Where were you when I laid the foundation
> > > of the earth?
> > Tell me, if you have understanding.
> > Who determined its measurements—surely
> > > you know!" (Job 38:1-5)

And on it goes for the next four chapters, with God bombarding Job with question after question: Have you commanded the morning and the dawn to appear each day since the beginning? Have you taken a stroll in the deepest oceans? Can you send forth lightning and hail and rain and thunder at your whim? Can you catch the mighty Leviathan of the sea on a fishhook and play with him as with a bird? Do you know all the secrets of life and death, and darkness and light?

The point is very clear: God is the supreme, majestic, sovereign ruler of the world; who are we to question him? Job understands this in the end:

> "I know that you can do all things,
>   and that no purpose of yours can be thwarted.
> 'Who is this that hides counsel without knowledge?'
> Therefore I have uttered what I did not understand,
>   things too wonderful for me, which I did not
>   know." (Job 42:2-3)

If no purpose of God's can be thwarted—if he will do what he will do, regardless of the questionings or actions of puny humanity—then what place could prayer have?

We see the answer in the very next paragraph:

> After the Lord had spoken these words to Job, the Lord said to Eliphaz the Temanite: "My anger burns against you and against your two friends, for you have not spoken of me what is right, as my servant Job has. Now therefore take seven bulls and seven rams and go to my servant Job and offer up a burnt offering for yourselves. And my servant Job shall pray for you, for I will accept his prayer not to deal with you according to your folly. For you have not

spoken of me what is right, as my servant Job has."
So Eliphaz the Temanite and Bildad the Shuhite
and Zophar the Naamathite went and did what the
Lord had told them, and the Lord accepted Job's
prayer. (Job 42:7-9)

Notice what happens here. God knows in advance that
Job will pray for his three friends and he tells Eliphaz
about it. Job then prays, as God said he would. And
then God accepts Job's prayer and forgives the three
friends their folly.

Could God have forgiven the three friends without
Job's prayer? Given what has just been said in the
previous four chapters, the answer must be, 'Yes'! God
doesn't need anyone to help him do anything, least of
all Job.

All the same, God does use Job's prayer as the
means for his forgiveness of the three friends. He
involves Job in the process—not because he has to and
not because he is otherwise powerless, but because, in
his sovereignty and grace and wisdom, he chooses to.
(For a similar example, see the way God uses
Abraham's prayer to heal Abimelech in Gen 20:6-17.)

God doesn't need our prayers in order to bless us or
other people. He knows what we need before we ask
him, as Jesus points out (Matt 6:7-8). But, in his
incredible kindness, he uses our prayers as a vehicle
or conduit for doing his work. It's much the same as
anything else we do for God in this world. Does God
need us—frail, weak, imperfect people that we are—in

order bring the gospel to people and see them converted? Of course not. God could speak directly to everyone, as he did to the Apostle Paul on the Damascus Road. But he chooses nonetheless to involve us in his great gospel project for the world. He uses our mouths and voices and hands and feet. He uses us as his ambassadors and teachers and encouragers. He grants us the extraordinary status of 'fellow workers' (see 1 Cor 3:5-9).

In the same way, we are God's fellow workers in prayer. God includes and uses our prayers in his purposes, much as a patient mother will let her three-year-old help with the cooking, even though it takes much longer and produces considerably more mess! God gathers our prayers into his purposes for our sake—to help us learn to trust him and depend upon him for all things.

This is why sometimes we "do not have" when we "do not ask". God makes many wonderful promises and he has many blessings in store for us, but he may deny us these blessings when we fail to ask for them. He has designed prayer as the means by which we grab hold of his blessings and promises and make them our own. John Calvin, the 16th-century Reformer, expressed this delightfully when he wrote:

> ... to know God as the master and bestower of all
> good things, who invites us to request them of him,
> and still not go to him and not ask of him—this
> would be of as little profit as for a man to neglect
> a treasure, buried and hidden in the earth, after it

had been pointed out to him ... It is, therefore, by the benefit of prayer that we reach those riches which are laid up for us with the Heavenly Father ... we dig up by prayer the treasures that were pointed out by the Lord's gospel, and which our faith has gazed upon.[3]

God has graciously ordained prayer as the means by which we dig up the riches he has promised us in the gospel. And he has done this for our sake—that we might learn to trust him, to flee to him in all our troubles, to overflow with gratitude when he grants our requests, and to appreciate even more the kindness and goodness he shows towards us. Calvin concludes by saying:

On account of these things, our most merciful Father, although he never either sleeps or idles, still very often gives the impression of one sleeping or idling in order that he may thus train us, otherwise idle and lazy, to seek, ask, and entreat him to our great good.[4]

---

[3] John Calvin, *Institutes of the Christian Religion*, translated by F. L. Battles, *Library of Christian Classics*, The Westminster Press, Philadelphia, 1960 III.20.1-2.

[4] *Institutes*, III.20.3.

WHAT HAPPENS WHEN WE PRAY?

Chapter 9

THE FELLOWSHIP OF PRAYER

As a rule, whenever Christianity has been strong, and the gospel has been growing and bearing fruit, believers have been united in labouring hard at prayer. The evangelical revival of the 18th century in England is famous for the conversion of thousands, for the powerful preaching of George Whitefield and John Wesley, and for the hymn-writing of Charles Wesley, John Newton and others. Yet it is not so often remembered that the incredible outpouring of God's grace at this time was also accompanied by a profound commitment to prayer on the part of ordinary Christians.

We catch a glimpse of this in a famous hymn of the period, 'Jesus, Where'er Thy People Meet'. It was written by the brilliant but troubled William Cowper.

Cowper, who suffered from bouts of severe depression and even insanity, was a friend and neighbour to John Newton (of 'Amazing Grace' fame).

Newton had organized weekly prayer meetings in the town of Olney where he was ministering, and a growing number of people were attending. "They have removed the prayer meeting to the great room in the Great House", Newton wrote. "It is a noble place, with a parlour behind it, and holds one hundred and thirty people conveniently."

This new and larger meeting-place for prayer prompted Newton to send a prayer request to a friend: "Pray for us, that the Lord may be in the midst of us there, and that as he has now given us a Rehoboth (a Hebrew word meaning 'a broad place or room'), and has made room for us, so that he may be pleased to add to our numbers, and make us fruitful in the land".

William Cowper was a member of this growing prayer group meeting in the great room of the Great House, and it was this experience that led to his writing of this great hymn. As you read the words (below), note how they touch on so many of the biblical truths of prayer we have been considering in this book: the character of the powerful, holy, merciful God as the basis for prayer; the sweetness of the access to himself which God grants us through Christ; the motivations and reasons for prayer (including God's command to pray); and the power and urgency of prayer to dig up the riches of God's blessing, both for ourselves and for others:

Jesus, where'er Thy people meet,
There they behold Thy mercy seat;
Where'er they see Thee Thou art found,
And every place is hallowed ground.

For Thou, within no walls confined,
Inhabitest the humble mind;
Such ever bring Thee, where they come,
And, going, take Thee to their home.

Dear Shepherd of Thy chosen few,
Thy former mercies here renew;
Here, to our waiting hearts, proclaim
The sweetness of Thy saving Name.

Here may we prove the power of prayer
To strengthen faith and sweeten care;
To teach our faint desires to rise,
And bring all Heav'n before our eyes.

Behold at Thy commanding word,
We stretch the curtain and the cord;
Come Thou, and fill this wider space,
And bless us with a large increase.

Lord, we are few, but Thou art near;
Nor short Thine arm, nor deaf Thine ear;
O rend the heavens, come quickly down,
And make a thousand hearts Thine own!

(William Cowper, 1769)

It's a delightful hymn to sing when you have just moved into a spacious new building for prayer, for it does not sit content with the delights of the 'great room' with its parlour behind. It recognizes that God is not confined to a room, but dwells by his Spirit in our hearts. It's only a special room because people with God in their hearts have come to it. God will be with them when they go home as well.

We do not often sing verse 5 these days, with its reference to praying at God's command. But we can imagine the faithful friends at Olney, few though they were, praying together in the Great House, pleading with God to fill this new 'wider space' with a large increase of friends to join them in prayer.

Charles Wesley wished that he had not one tongue but a thousand tongues with which to sing his great Redeemer's praise. William Cowper's wish was for God to "make a thousand hearts Thine own". And through the preaching of Newton, Whitefield, Wesley, Grimshaw and many others, God did all that and more.

What Cowper also beautifully expresses is that prayer not only springs from and expresses our fellowship with the Father through the Son in the Spirit, it also takes place within the fellowship of believers. Prayer is a privilege we can enjoy together and a struggle in which we can help each other.

Christians have always met together to pray. From the earliest days of the church in Acts, we see that the disciples "with one accord were devoting themselves to prayer" as they waited in Jerusalem for the Holy Spirit to be sent to them from the risen Christ (Acts 1:14). And after Pentecost, as the new community of Christ flourished and grew, prayer was a constant feature:

> And they devoted themselves to the apostles'
> teaching and fellowship, to the breaking of bread
> and the **prayers**. (Acts 2:42)

> When [Peter and John] were released, they went to
> their friends and reported what the chief priests and
> the elders had said to them. And when they heard it,
> **they lifted their voices together to God** and said,
> "Sovereign Lord, who made the heaven and the earth
> and the sea and everything in them ..." (Acts 4:23-24)

> And when they had **prayed**, the place in which they
> were gathered together was shaken, and they were
> all filled with the Holy Spirit and continued to
> speak the word of God with boldness. (Acts 4:31)

We see indications of the same in 1 Corinthians where corporate prayer was clearly a regular part of the Christian gathering (1 Cor 11:4-5; 14:13-17). And in his first letter to Timothy, Paul expresses his desire that the men of the congregation would pray together without anger or quarrelling (1 Tim 2:8).[1]

---

[1] The NIV's unfortunate translation of this verse—"I want men everywhere to lift up holy hands in prayer, without anger or disputing"—makes it sound as if Paul's primary command is for men to lift up their hands. The emphasis in the original is on the prayer, as the ESV translation reflects: "I desire then that in every place the men should pray, lifting holy hands without anger or quarrelling" (see also NRSV and NASB).

There is a danger, of course, in praying publicly with other Christians. We may be tempted to put on a performance to impress them. Jesus warned his disciples about just this sort of hypocrisy:

"And when you pray, you must not be like the hypocrites. For they love to stand and pray in the synagogues and at the street corners, that they may be seen by others. Truly, I say to you, they have received their reward. But when you pray, go into your room and shut the door and pray to your Father who is in secret. And your Father who sees in secret will reward you." (Matt 6:5-6)

As with giving to the poor and fasting (the other subjects mentioned in Matthew 6), we must do our righteous deeds to please our heavenly Father, not other people. If God sees everything and knows everything, then what is to be gained by praying loudly and prominently in public on the street corner? It doesn't make it any easier for God to see or hear. It can only be so that **others** can see and be suitably impressed at our righteousness.

This is certainly an error to be avoided, but one suspects it is hardly the main problem for most modern Christians. Our struggle is that we pray **hardly at all**, not that we pray too prominently and publicly in order to gain kudos for ourselves.

For those who are struggling in prayer and who feel like giving up, the fellowship of other Christians is a blessing. Our brothers and sisters can remind us to pray and spur us on to pray—with their words, with their own example of prayerfulness and also simply by agreeing to pray with us at an appointed time.

The fellowship of prayer is a gift from God.

A final challenge

More than once in this book, we have dipped into the epistle of James to see the nature and importance of prayer. As we conclude, we would do well to ponder another passage in James's challenging little letter.

In chapter 1, verse 21, we find what is probably the key verse of the whole epistle:

> Therefore put away all filthiness and rampant wickedness and **receive with meekness the implanted word**, which is able to save your souls.

This "implanted word" is the 'word of truth', the gospel which brings us to new birth and is able to save our souls (see vv. 17-18). The many practical down-to-earth exhortations, for which James is famous, all flow from this, because **to receive God's word with meekness and humility is to put it into practice in our lives**. To accept it is to obey it. And that's what James goes on to urge upon us in the verses immediately following:

> But be doers of the word, and not hearers only, deceiving yourselves. For if anyone is a hearer of

the word and not a doer, he is like a man who looks intently at his natural face in a mirror. For he looks at himself and goes away and at once forgets what he was like. But the one who looks into the perfect law, the law of liberty, and perseveres, being no hearer who forgets but a doer who acts, he will be blessed in his doing. (Jas 1:22-25)

We hear the word and it strikes a chord of truth in us. We feel that mix of excitement and satisfaction that comes from realizing that, yes, this does describe the true state of things. This is what I am like and this is what I must now do—like a man who stares at himself in a mirror for the first time in weeks and realizes with a shock that he desperately needs a haircut.

But if the process stops with listening to the word—even listening intently to it—then we have not 'received the word' at all. This is the terrible self-delusion of the Sunday Christian who goes to church for years and hears hundreds of sermons, but never truly repents and puts his faith in Christ. He may believe that, by going to church and listening thoughtfully to the word, he has improved himself and won favour with God and man. But as soon as he walks out the church door, his spiritual state of mind evaporates, he forgets what he has heard, and he goes about his business for another week as he always does. For all his gazing in the mirror, his hair remains uncut.

By contrast, the person who puts the word into effect, "being no hearer who forgets but a doer who acts", is blessed. He hears and realizes that the word of God calls for action and response, for repentance and faith, for discipleship and self-denial. He understands that to accept God's word with a humble and contrite heart must lead to action, and he perseveres in taking that action.

The application of all this to prayer is obvious. To learn about prayer but not to pray is a waste of time. Worse, it is self-delusion, for we fool ourselves into thinking that because we have read about prayer and have been convinced of the importance of prayer and have even felt guilty about our lack of prayer, we have actually done something about prayer. Let us not deceive ourselves into thinking that by reading a book on prayer we have actually improved our prayer lives.

Of course, by reading this book, you have done something useful. You've gazed intently into God's word and been taught about prayer—what it is, why we should do it, why we don't do it and how we can do it. You have (hopefully) been stirred and stimulated and convicted and moved to pray. But what remains now is to be a doer who acts rather than a self-deceived hearer who goes away and forgets.

Now would be a good time to stop and consider what practical steps you are going to take to put God's word about prayer into action. When are you planning to put aside regular time for prayer? What do you need to change in order for this to happen?

When will you start?

Chapter 10

SEVEN COMMON QUESTIONS

OVER THE YEARS, AS WE'VE preached, conducted seminars and group discussions, and spoken with individuals, various questions about prayer keep arising. We've covered a number of them in the text of the book, but here are seven common questions which are worth a few extra words.

1. My prayer life is virtually non-existent. I don't even feel like a Christian any more. What can I do?

Nearly all Christians go through periods where they give up praying—that is, their regular habit of prayer is interrupted by illness or family crisis or busyness or just plain laziness, and they don't get around to re-establishing it. The daily prayer time goes out the window and, after a period of stuttering stops and starts, we wake up one morning and realize that it has been a week, two weeks, a month, or longer since we have stopped and prayed on our own to God.

There is only one word for this process: sin. And like so much sin, it happens not with a bang but with a whimper. It steals upon us slowly, like the relaxing cloud of sleep that descends on Sunday afternoons if we sit too long in the armchair. Let's not excuse it or paint it with pastels; it's terribly wrong.

Prayerlessness is sin, and the Bible warns us how easy it is to deceive ourselves about sin in two quite different ways.

On the one hand, we can pretend to ourselves that there isn't really a problem—that we're not sinning and that we don't need to worry about it. But this is self-deception. The Christian life is a constant battle between flesh and Spirit, and the flesh will sometimes have its way, this side of glory (Gal 5:16-25). The Christian life is not an effortless, glorious, upward cruise of victory over sin; it is a hard-fought battle, with much stumbling and falling, and much repenting and begging for forgiveness.

Christians of tender conscience who are cut to the heart at their failure to pray, and who doubt their salvation as a result, need to remember this truth. Failure is our unwelcome but constant companion on the Christian walk. The very fact that we are experiencing the battle against sin (and, in this instance, getting a bloody nose) is an indication that we're in a fight. It is quite right that our prayerlessness should make us feel guilty and that we should long to put it right. But it should not lead us to doubt the faithfulness and mercy of our Master. We may be faithless at times, but he is supremely faithful and will cleanse us from all unrighteousness (1 John 1:9).

However, we can also be deceived in the opposite direction by thinking that our prayerlessness doesn't matter. "After all," we may say to ourselves, "once a Christian, always a Christian. God has paid for my sins. And besides, even if I don't pray, he will still fulfil his sovereign will." If we are sliding into this way of thinking, Scripture has a strong message for us:

> Do you not know that the unrighteous will not inherit the kingdom of God? Do not be deceived: neither the sexually immoral, nor idolaters, nor adulterers, nor men who practice homosexuality, nor thieves, nor the greedy, nor drunkards, nor revilers, nor swindlers will inherit the kingdom of God. And such were some of you. But you were washed, you were sanctified, you were justified in the name of the Lord Jesus Christ and by the Spirit of our God. (1 Cor 6:9-11)

Persistent, unrepentant ungodliness will exclude us from the kingdom of God. We cannot and must not presume upon God, thinking that our sin doesn't matter. We will find out one day, to our cost, that it matters a great deal. We must repent of our prayerlessness and start again. Christianity is a start-again life.

2. I want to kick-start my prayer life but I don't know how. Do you have any suggestions?

If you're at the point of starting (or re-starting) a life of regular prayer, here are some practical ideas to help you get going:

1. Repent of your prayerlessness. Confess your failings to your heavenly Father. Don't hold back. We may sometimes deceive ourselves, but he is never fooled. Ask God to forgive you and to work in you by his Spirit to enable you to change.

2. Devise a simple, not-too-ambitious pattern of regular prayer that fits with your lifestyle. Don't resolve to have 'a two-hour prayer time' every morning before breakfast. The length of time will not impress God and it will most likely discourage you (when you fail to meet it). Start with a regular, manageable program—for example, a time of prayer every night before bed, or a regular slot at lunch time, or a walk before breakfast during which you pray.

3. Work out what you are going to do when you pray. For example, you might use the time-honoured, simple, but very effective method of reading a short passage of Scripture and, from the passage, picking out one thing to give thanks for, one thing to ask God's forgiveness for, and one other request to bring to God. You can apply these three points to yourself, your family and others you wish to pray for. You might even jot down a list of

people and apply these prayer points to a different one each day. Another simple way to pray is to use the Lord's Prayer as a kind of template. (See Appendix i for some useful summaries of what to pray for, including how to use the Lord's Prayer in your prayers.)

4. With a regular pattern decided upon and a simple method to use, work hard at keeping to this pattern for 4-6 weeks. During this time, don't try to do anything too fancy or different. Just focus on establishing (or re-establishing) a regular habit of prayer in your life. Habits are powerful and, if they are good habits, very useful. Of course, we should be wary of turning a prayer habit into a meaningless daily ritual—a kind of legalistic 'good work' that we have to perform in order to stay in God's good books. Habits are best thought of as alarm clocks. Once established, they wake us up at a certain time each day and say, "Time to pray!" They are a helpful device for sleepy, sinful people like us, who by nature would much rather do anything than pray.

5. Tell someone. Just as habits are helpful weapons in our battle against our own laziness and unbelief, so too is Christian fellowship. Ask a friend to pray for you as you commit yourself to regular personal prayer. You might even find that your friend is struggling too, and that you can encourage and urge each other to stick to a plan of action.

6. Once you've established a regular habit, you can branch out and do more. Extend your regular time, or think about other times of the day or other regular occasions when you might pray. When you've been talking to someone on the phone, pause for a minute or two after you hang up to pray for them. If you're chatting to someone at church and they share something with you, stop right then and there and pray with the person for a few minutes. The possibilities are endless. I know two elderly sisters who live alone in different parts of the city. They call each other every night, have a chat about the day and then pray together over the phone.

These are all just suggestions, not law. The important thing is that we heed God's call to pray, that we confess our stupidity and sinfulness in failing to pray, and that we get back on our knees again and again.

3. What is 'praying in the Spirit'?

Twice in the New Testament, we are urged to pray in the Holy Spirit. Here are the two references:

In all circumstances take up the shield of faith, with which you can extinguish all the flaming darts of the evil one; and take the helmet of salvation, and the sword of the Spirit, which is the word of God, **praying at all times in the Spirit**, with all prayer and supplication. To that end keep alert with all perseverance, making supplication for all the saints ... (Eph 6:16-18)

[19] It is these who cause divisions, worldly people, devoid of the Spirit. [20] But you, beloved, building yourselves up in your most holy faith, and **praying in the Holy Spirit,** [21] keep yourselves in the love of God, waiting for the mercy of our Lord Jesus Christ that leads to eternal life. (Jude 19-21, authors' translation)

What does this mean? Is this 'Spirit prayer' a special kind of prayer—prayer on a higher plane?

The context of both passages shows that praying 'in the Spirit' is indeed special and extraordinary, but it is not a super-charged mode of prayer that is only sometimes achieved. 'Praying in the Spirit' is the amazing privilege of all true Christian prayer.

In Ephesians 6:18, Paul urges his readers to pray "at all times in the Spirit". This immediately rules out the suggestion made by some that 'praying in the Spirit' is a reference to some special kind of prayer, like speaking in tongues. It is very clear from what Paul says elsewhere that not all Christians have the gift of 'speaking in tongues', whatever that gift might be (1 Cor 12:30; 14:26-27). And so, in urging all the Ephesians to pray "at all times in the Spirit", Paul cannot be referring to a practice that only some Christians are gifted to undertake.

The rest of the passage, and indeed the rest of Ephesians, make clear what Paul is referring to. The

Spirit is the seal of our heavenly inheritance (1:13-14), who grants us access to the Father (2:18), builds us into a dwelling place fit for God (2:22), strengthens us with power in our inner being (3:16), unites us with other Christians (4:3-4), and fills us so that we can live a godly, wise life, full of thanksgiving (5:18-21). The whole Christian life is "in the Spirit", even the daily spiritual battle described in chapter 6. One of our weapons is the sword of the Spirit—the word of God— and the prayers we undertake in the midst of the fight are also "in the Spirit". It is only in and by God's work within us—by his Spirit dwelling in us—that we can come before him, have access to him as beloved children, and wage war against the spiritual powers of evil that constantly seek to weaken our faith, disrupt our obedience, and lessen our grasp on the truth.

The message of Jude is remarkably similar. In the face of worldly scoffers who follow their own passions and cause divisions, and who are "devoid of the Spirit", Jude urges his readers to stay true. They are to keep themselves in the love of God (21), and the way they are to do it is by building themselves up in the holy faith and praying in the Holy Spirit (20). This is simply a different way of describing the Christian battle of Ephesians 6. In our struggle against all that opposes us as God's people, we need to keep building and rebuilding our trust in God, and keep praying to him in the strength of the Holy Spirit he has given us.

4. Does the quantity of our faith affect our prayers?

Sometimes, when we don't get the answer in prayer that we were hoping for, we are tempted to think that the problem is our faith. If only we had believed a little harder—a little stronger—a little more fervently—then God would have given us what we asked for. In other words, we sometimes think that faith is like a muscle with which we push God. And if we could only push a bit harder, then God would give way and grant our requests.

But this is not what 'faith' is. As we've already seen in chapter 2, faith is active trust or reliance or dependence upon someone. It's relying on the lifesaver to get you back to the shore. Now the really crucial thing in your rescue is not how much trust you have in the lifesaver, but whether the lifesaver is strong and skilful enough to get you back to shore. The important thing about faith is the **object** of your faith, not how much faith you might have. As Jesus said to his disciples when they asked him to 'increase their faith',

> "If you had faith like a grain of mustard seed, you
> could say to this mulberry tree, 'Be uprooted and
> planted in the sea,' and it would obey you." (Luke 17:6)

If we are praying for something and God doesn't grant our request, it may be that his will for us is otherwise. Or it may be that he is teaching us to be patient. But if we are expressing our confidence and trust in God by calling upon him in prayer, then the quantity of our faith is not the issue.

5. What about when I just don't feel like praying?

Sometimes we don't feel at all like praying. Is it phoney or inauthentic to press ahead and pray when our hearts are not in it? Or should we wait until we feel more 'in the mood' for prayer?

If prayer were a mystical activity that required a certain kind or level of feeling to succeed, then our 'mood' would be very important. But prayer is not mystical contact with the divine; it's asking God for things—constantly, regularly, on all occasions.

One day, in the eternal kingdom of God, we will always feel like praying. Thanks and trust will flow out from us like fragrance from a flower. But in the meantime, our feelings about prayer will be mixed, because we ourselves are 'mixed'. We have God's Spirit within us, but we still live in the flesh and we still battle against the desires of the flesh—one of which is to neglect prayer!

Thus, whether our hearts feel cold and lifeless, or despairing and depressed, or happy and satisfied, or anxious and fearful, or bored and tired, or angry and upset, or joyous and glad—in any and every circumstance of life, regardless of how we feel, we should come before our Father and pour out our thanksgiving to him for all his mercies, and bring our requests to him in expression of our trust in his goodness. This is the command of God to us for our good, and we should obey it. God knows the fickleness of our hearts and our feelings. He urges us to keep praying, regardless of how we feel—not only because in so doing we grab hold of his blessings, but because we very often improve the way we feel as a result! 'Feeling like praying' often comes as we pray and after we pray, rather than before.

6. Jesus says that "whatever you ask in prayer, believe that you have received it, and it will be yours" (Mark 11:24). Does that mean if I ask for something and don't receive it, my lack of faith is to blame?

To answer this question and to find out what Jesus' words mean, we must remember two important, time-honoured principles of Bible reading:

1. Be careful of quoting texts out of context. Read the rest of the chapter (and more) from which the quote comes.
2. Don't read one part of Scripture in such a way that it contradicts another.

In this case, the context tells us quite a lot about what Jesus' words mean and don't mean. In Mark 11, Jesus has just entered Jerusalem in triumph to the cries of "Hosanna! Blessed is he who comes in the name of the Lord!" Yet when he looks around at what's happening in Jerusalem, he doesn't like what he sees (such as the money-changers in the temple). As the story proceeds, it becomes very clear that Jerusalem is in a sad state: barren, faithless and unwilling to accept her Lord when he visits her.

This is the bigger story that makes sense of the cursing of the fig tree, which is where Jesus makes his statement about prayer:

> [20] As they passed by in the morning, they saw the fig tree withered away to its roots. [21] And Peter remembered and said to him, "Rabbi, look! The fig tree that you cursed has withered." [22] And Jesus answered them, "Have faith in God. [23] Truly, I say to you, whoever says to this mountain, 'Be taken up and thrown into the sea,' and does not doubt in his heart, but believes that what he says will come to pass, it will be done for him. [24] **Therefore I tell you, whatever you ask in prayer, believe that you have received it, and it will be yours.** [25] And whenever you stand praying, forgive, if you have anything against anyone, so that your Father also who is in heaven may forgive you your trespasses." (Mark 11:20-25)

The fig tree is an Old Testament image of the prosperity of Israel and her enjoyment of God's blessing. When things are going really swimmingly in Israel, each man "[sits] under his vine and under his fig tree" (e.g. 1 Kings 4:25). Conversely, when Israel is being judged for her rebellion against God, the fig tree is withered and fruitless. (Take a look at the stinging prophecy of Jeremiah 8:4-13 as a classic example.)

The context of Jesus' remark about prayer is frightening. The King is coming to his city, Jerusalem, but he finds it rebellious and apostate. The result can only be cursing, not blessing—the fearful judgement foretold by the prophets. There will be salvation springing from this judgement, but the judgement will be awful. When Jesus refers to "this mountain" being thrown into the sea, he seems to be alluding to Zechariah's prophecy. He has to come Jerusalem as her king, "humble and mounted on a donkey" (Zech 9:9), and soon he will become "him whom they have pierced" (Zech 12 :10). In Mark 11, Jesus refers back to Zechariah 14 in which the Mount of Olives ("this mountain") is split in two on the terrible day in which God comes to judge his people.

How does this context help us understand Jesus' promise about 'whatever we ask'?

- Jesus' illustration of 'removing mountains' is not a random impossible feat—as if he had said, "If anyone says to this lake, 'Be drained and filled with milk instead' it will be done for him". In the context of Mark 11 and Jesus' coming to faithless Jerusalem, the prayer for "this mountain" to be overthrown is a prayer for Judgement Day—for the kingdom of God. It is asking that, in line with his promise, God would judge his faithless, disobedient people and bring in his kingdom. Jesus' reassurance that God will most certainly answer this prayer is no different from what we have seen elsewhere in the Bible's teaching about prayer—that, if we pray for the desires of God, we can be sure he will grant our request in his own good and wise time.

- This also makes sense of verse 25. If the kind of prayer Jesus is talking about has to do with God's judgement, then it would also be about forgiveness. This is also something we can confidently bring to God, because he has promised that in the midst of judgement he will forgive those who repent and put their trust in him—provided of course that we really do want forgiveness and are committed to forgiveness (as demonstrated by our commitment to forgiving others; see our discussion of this in chapter 6).

- Verse 25 also shows that the promise of verse 24 is not a 'blank cheque' for receiving absolutely anything we ask for if we believe hard enough. If I am a merciless person who refuses to forgive others, then it doesn't matter how earnest and believing I am; I cannot expect to receive forgiveness from God until I repent of my unforgiving spirit.

When we combine this understanding with what we know elsewhere from the Scriptures about prayer, it's clear that Jesus is not promising a 'blank cheque' if only we have enough faith. He is promising that God will fulfil his plans for judgement and salvation. Our response should be to put all our trust in him, to pray that his judgement would come, and to pray for forgiveness when judgement comes. These are prayers God will most certainly answer.

7. Surely we shouldn't eliminate 'listening to God' from prayer? Surely in our relationship with God there must be listening as well as speaking?

This question is actually a different question in disguise. All Christians agree that we must listen to God as well as speak to him. In fact, it's impossible to be a Christian without listening to God's word, the gospel, and putting our trust in him.

What this question is really about is whether listening to God should be confined to listening to the message of the Scriptures as we read them, study them, and share them with each other. Those who want to 'listen to God in prayer' are really making an argument for God speaking to individual Christians outside and beyond the Scriptures, through impressions, inner voices and promptings of the Holy Spirit.

This book is not the place to answer that question in detail. If you're interested, we have argued elsewhere that God's word to us in the Scriptures is his final, complete and sufficient revelation of himself through Jesus Christ in these last days in which we live.[1] But whatever view you take of how God speaks to us, his speaking to us and our listening to him is not 'prayer'. It's the wrong label.

In the Bible, prayer is asking God for things. It is

---

[1]   Phillip D. Jensen and Tony Payne, *Guidance and the Voice of God*, Matthias Media, Sydney, 1997.

depending upon God in all things by asking him for all things, knowing that he will keep his promise to grant us every good gift. Prayer is not listening to God's voice; it is responding to God's voice.

Appendix i

A SUMMARY TO LOOK BACK OVER

IN CHAPTER 9, WE CONSIDERED the danger of getting all fired up about prayer by reading this book, but then doing nothing about it—like the fool in James 1 who sees his face in the mirror but then goes away and forgets what he looks like.

One way to stop ourselves forgetting is to go back over what we've learnt; to revise, and ponder, and be stimulated again to pray.

To help you do this easily, we've put together a little point-form summary of the most important points of this book—especially those that motivate us to keep praying, and that give us ideas about how to pray and what to pray for.

So when your prayer life starts to flag, or you find

yourself stuck for things to pray, pull out this summary and remind yourself of all the powerful reasons there are to pray, all the dangerous lies that stop us from praying, and all the many wonderful things there are to pray about.

The summary is organized under four headings:

1. Why we pray
2. Why we don't pray
3. How to pray
4. What to pray for

1. Why we pray

a. The God of prayer

We should pray because of who God is (chapter 2):

- God is **able** to do all things (Ps 33).
- God is our **Father** and he is willing to care for us and give us good things (Acts 17:24-28; Ps 104:13-15, 21-24, 27-28).
- God is a God who **speaks and listens**, unlike idols who cannot do either (Ps 115:2-8).
- God is **holy** and therefore unapproachable (1 Tim 6:16; Isa 59:1-2).
- God is **merciful** and provides the means by which we can come before him in prayer (Heb 9:11-14; 10:19-22).

b. Why we should pray

We should pray because of our relationship with God (chapter 3):

- We pray because, in his great mercy, **God allows us to**; because as a loving Father he has adopted us as his children, and given us free access to his throne.
- We pray because **we must**—because we are sinners and we are completely dependent on him (1 John 1:7-2:2).
- We pray because **we are commanded to** and therefore not to pray is disobedience and sin (Eph 6:17-18; 1 Thess 5:16-18; Rom 12:12; Col 4:2).
- We pray because of **God's promise** to hear and answer our prayers (Ps 50:15; Matt 7:7-11).

2. Why we don't pray

We don't pray because:

a. We have false views of God

- We doubt whether God is able to act in response to our prayers:
  - We think God is limited by the fixed natural laws he has put in place to govern our world (compare with Jer 32:17).
  - We think God is limited by his fixed, unchangeable sovereign will (compare with Exod 32:9-14; Jer 26:19).

- We question whether God is willing to act for our benefit.
  - We question God's willingness because of the problem of evil (but God is able to act despite and through evil, e.g. Acts 2:23, and he does not always answer us in the way we expect).
  - We think our requests may be too small or insignificant to warrant his attention (yet God is very interested in even the minute details of our lives, e.g. Matt 10:29-31).

b. We have false views of our relationship with God
- We do not trust God and we persist in disobedience (Heb 3:15-19; Isa 1:15).
- We think that our prayers have only been heard when we receive what we have asked for or because we have prayed in a certain way.
- We think our feelings are an indication of the quality of our prayers or whether God has heard us.

c. Sin and Satan
- Because we are sinful, we don't want to rely on God, or respond to his call.
- Our adversary, the Devil, doesn't want us to pray (Jas 4:7-8; 1 Pet 5:6-8).

3. How to pray

Prayer is not a matter of technique but of relationship (chapter 5). However:

- Our prayers should be made up of **words**, spoken by us to God.
  - ○ Prayer is not listening to God.
  - ○ Prayer is not meditation.
- The best time for prayer is **any time and at all times**.
  - ○ Length doesn't matter; the length of our prayers does not affect God's answer (Matt 6:7).
  - ○ Physical posture doesn't matter but our spiritual posture should be repentant and humble (Isa 66:1-2).
- We should pray according to **biblical foundations**:
  - ○ We pray as dependent sons (Gal 4:4-7).
  - ○ We pray by the Spirit (Rom 8:13-17).
  - ○ We pray through the Son (1 Tim 2:5-6).
  - ○ We pray to the Father (Matt 6:9).
  - ○ We pray with thanksgiving (Phil 4:6).
  - ○ We pray with difficulty—because of sin (Gal 5:16-17).

4. What to pray for

a. Prayers from Scripture to use as models for your own prayers

Prayers in the Old Testament:

- David (2 Sam 7:18-29; Pss 17, 39, 51, 55, 61, 86, 102, 142);
- Solomon (1 Kgs 3:6-9; 8:22-53; 2 Chr 6:13-42);
- Hezekiah (2 Kgs 19:14-19; Isa 37:14-20);
- Ezra (Ezra 9:5-15);
- Nehemiah (Neh 1:4-11);
- The Levites (Neh 9:5-38);
- Agur (Prov 30);
- Isaiah (Isa 63:15-64:12);
- Daniel (Dan 9:3-19).

The prayers of Jesus:

- Matthew 6:9-13;
- Mark 14:35-36;
- John 17.

The prayers of Paul:

- Romans 15:5-6;
- Ephesians 1:15-23; 3:14-21;
- Philippians 1:9-11;
- Colossians 1:9-14;
- 1 Thessalonians 3:9-13; 5:23-24;
- 2 Thessalonians 1:11-12; 2:16-17.

b. What to pray

i. We can pray according to what God desires (chapter 6):

- We can pray about his **plans** for us in Christ:
  - That all things be united under Christ (Eph 1:3-10);
  - That we be conformed to the image of his son (Rom 8:28-30);
  - That we become part of a new people who are purified from their sin and zealous for good works (Titus 2:11-14);
  - That we stand firm and live in holiness, and finally obtain the glory of our Lord Jesus Christ (2 Thess 2:13-15; 1 Thess 4:1-3).

- We can pray about his **promises**:
  - He will give wisdom to all who ask (Jas 1:5);
  - He will not let us be tempted beyond our ability but will provide a way out (1 Cor 10:13);
  - He will forgive us our sins and cleanse us from all unrighteousness if we confess our sins (1 John 1:9);
  - There will be no mourning, crying or pain in the new creation (Rev 21:4);
  - Nothing can separate us from his love (Rom 8:37-39);
  - The pure of heart shall see God (Matt 5:8);
  - He will draw near if we draw near to him (Jas 4:8a);
  - He will sustain us if we cast our burdens upon him (Ps 55:22);

- He has removed our sins and cast them far away (Ps 103:12).
- We can pray about his **commands**—for example, the Ten Commandments (Exod 20:1-17), or Paul's instructions (e.g. Col 3:1-17).
- We can pray according to the Lord's Prayer (Matt 6:9-13; Luke 11:2-4):
  - for his name to be revered and honoured as the mighty Saviour;
  - for his kingdom to come in all its fullness;
  - for his kingdom to extend here and now throughout the world in the lives of people as they submit to his rule;
  - for his people to taste the blessings of that kingdom now;
  - for him to forgive our sins and for us to live by forgiveness;
  - for him to deliver us from the evil one and his testings.

ii. *We can pray about the anxieties of life (chapter 7):*
- There is nothing too small to bring before God (Phil 4:6; Matt 6:25-34).
- The more our hearts and minds are changed by the work of God's word and Spirit, the more our prayers will reflect God's own mind (Rom 12:2).
- We should pray with thanksgiving (Phil 4:6) because it brings God glory, and therefore stops

us from taking him for granted, and it lifts our spirits and changes our perspective.

- We should remember that God knows what we need, so we can trust him completely (Rom 8:26-27).

Appendix ii

DISCUSSION
GUIDE

THE QUESTIONS THAT FOLLOW ARE designed to make it
easy for small groups to discuss the content of *Prayer and
the Voice of God*, with their Bibles open. Feel free to pick
and choose your way through the questions (and references), depending on how much time you have available.

You can work through the discussion guide one
chapter per session (10 sessions) or by combining some
of the chapters as follows (6 sessions):

   i.   chapters 1 and 2
   ii. chapters 3 and 4
   iii. chapter 5
   iv. chapters 6 and 7
   v. chapter 8
   vi. chapters 9 and 10

Chapter 1: Prayer and God's voice

1. Before you started reading this chapter, how would you have defined 'prayer'?
2. What is prayer in the Bible? (You might like to look up some or all of these verses: Matt 6:9-13; 9:38; 21:22; 24:20; 26:41; Mark 11:24; 13:18; 14:35; 14:38; Luke 10:2; 11:2-4; 21:36; 22:40; 22:46; Acts 1:24.)
3. What **isn't** prayer?
4. The authors define prayer as "asking God for things". Do you agree?
5. List any questions you might have about prayer that you hope the book will address.
6. Pray about some of these things.

Chapter 2: The God of prayer

1. Read Psalm 33. Is there anything God is incapable of doing? What does this mean for our prayers?
2. What does it mean for our prayers if God is a fatherly provider to all? (See Acts 17:24-28 and Ps 104.)
3. How is God different to an idol (Ps 115:2-8)? What does this mean for our prayers?
4. What does God's holiness mean for our prayers? (See 1 Tim 6:16 and Isa 59:1-2.)
5. What does God's mercy mean for our prayers? (See Heb 9:11-14 and 10:19-22.)
6. What have you learnt about prayer from this chapter? How will this affect the way you pray?
7. Pray about some of these things.

Chapter 3: Why pray?

1. What is your motivation to pray?
2. Why does having access to approach God motivate us to pray?
3. Why is prayer necessary for our relationship with God (1 Jn 1:7-2:2)?
4. What is the purpose of the Bible's repeated commands to pray? What are the implications of not praying?
5. How does God's promise to hear our prayers (e.g. Ps 50:15; Matt 7:7-11) motivate us to pray?
6. What have you learnt about prayer from this chapter? How will this affect the way you pray?
7. Pray about some of these things.

Chapter 4: Why we don't pray

1. What sorts of things stop you from praying?
2. Why are false views of God and false views of our relationship with God so damaging to our prayer lives?
3. With regards to your life, is there anything that you feel God can't do (cf. Jer 32:17)?
4. When is it easy to doubt God's goodness, generosity and willingness to hear? Do Jesus' words in Mark 14:36 help us?
5. Why is prayerlessness disobedience (Heb 3:15-19)?
6. What are the dangers of:
   a. basing your view of whether God has heard your prayers on the results of those prayers?

    b. trusting in particular prayer positions or formulas to make God heed your prayers?

    c. using your feelings as a barometer of your relationship with God?

    d. letting yourself be distracted by Satan (cf. Jas 4:7-8; 1 Pet 5:6-8)?

7. What have you learnt about prayer from this chapter —particularly from the example of Jesus (Mark 14:32-50)? How will this affect the way you pray?

8. Pray about some of these things.

Chapter 5: How to pray

1. How do you pray? (Times of day, length, frequency, method, etc.)

2. "Prayer is not a matter of technique but of relationship." What do the authors mean by this? Do you agree?

3. According to God, what is the proper 'posture' for prayer (Isa 66:1-2; Ps 51:17)?

   The gospel is the foundation of prayer and from it, the Bible's teaching on how we pray can be summed up in six statements:

   a. We pray as dependent sons

   b. We pray by the Spirit

   c. We pray through the Son

   d. We pray to the Father

   e. We pray with thanksgiving

   f. We pray with difficulty

4. How does being adopted into God's family affect the way we pray (cf. Matt 7:9-11)?

5. What role does the Holy Spirit have in enabling us to pray? (See John 16:8; 14:16-17, 23; 1 Cor 12:3; Rom 8:13-17.)
6. Why do we pray through the Son?
7. If we are finding it difficult to pray, what are the possible reasons for this?
8. What freedoms do we have in how we pray? How would we respond to someone who tells us that we ought to pray in a particular way?
9. What have you learnt about prayer from this chapter? How will this affect the way you pray?
10. Pray about some of these things.

Chapter 6: The desires of God

1. How do you know what to pray for?
2. What does God desire for you in:
   a. his plans (Eph 1:3-10)? (See also Rom 8:28-30; Titus 2:11-14; 2 Thess 2:13-15; 1 Thess 4:1-3.)
   b. his promises? (See, for example, Pss 55:22; 103:12; Matt 5:8; Rom 8:37-39; 1 Cor 10:13; Jas 1:5; 4:8a; 1 John 1:9; Rev 21:4.)
   c. his commands? (See, for example, Exod 20:1-17; Matt 5-8; Phil 4:4-7.)
   d. the Lord's Prayer (Matt 6:9-13; Luke 11:2-4)?
3. Are these things what you want for yourself? Why/ why not?
4. What have you learnt about prayer from this chapter? How will this affect the way you pray?
5. Pray about some of these things.

Chapter 7: The anxieties of life

1. Think of a situation where you were faced with a problem or were anxious about something, and you weren't sure what God's will was. How did you work out what to pray?
2. Read Matthew 6:25-34. What does Jesus tell us to do with all our anxieties? Why?
3. How does your mind-set affect your prayers? What areas of your mind need 'renovating'?
4. What is the problem with the 'name it and claim it' attitude to prayer?
5. Why should we pray with thanksgiving (Phil 4:6)?
6. How does knowing that God knows what we need (Rom 8:26-27) help us in our prayers?
7. What have you learnt about prayer from this chapter? How will this affect the way you pray?
8. Pray about some of these things.

Chapter 8: What happens when we pray?

1. What are some of the reasons that we think God hasn't heard our prayers, or that our prayers don't make a difference? Are they valid reasons?
2. How can we be sure that God has heard us (1 John 5:14-15)?
3. What might God's response be if we pray:
   a. according to his desires?
   b. about the anxieties of life? (See also 2 Cor 12:7-9.)

4. Why must we approach God only 'in the name of Jesus'? (See also Heb 10:19-22.)

5. What are the consequences for our prayers if we cherish sin our hearts (Ps 66:18; Matt 6:14-15; Jas 4:2b-4)? Examine your own hearts to see if this is the case.

6. How does God's sovereignty interact with our prayers? What difference do our prayers make?

7. What have you learnt about prayer from this chapter? How will this affect the way you pray?

8. Pray about some of these things.

Chapter 9: The fellowship of prayer

1. What is the purpose of praying with others?

2. What are the dangers of praying with others (Matt 6:5-6)? What are the benefits of praying with others?

3. Look back over what you have read so far. What are the main points?

4. What are some of the things you have learnt about prayer from this book?

5. What is the danger of reading this book, learning all about prayer and not doing anything about it?

6. What practical steps are you going to take as a result of reading this book?

7. Pray about some of these things.

Chapter 10: Seven common questions

Look back over the questions you jotted down at the start. Do you have any more questions about prayer that are not covered in this section? Can you work out the answers to them from the rest of this book?

 **matthiasmedia**

Matthias Media is a ministry team of like-minded, evangelical Christians working together to achieve a particular goal, as summarized in our mission statement:

To serve our Lord Jesus Christ, and the growth of his gospel in the world, by producing and delivering high quality, Bible-based resources.

It was in 1988 that we first started pursuing this mission together, and in God's kindness we now have more than 250 different ministry resources being distributed all over the world. These resources range from Bible studies and books, through to training courses and audio sermons.

To find out more about our large range of very useful products, and to access samples and free downloads, visit our website:

www.matthiasmedia.com.au

How to purchase our resources
1. Through a range of outlets in various parts of the world. Visit **www.matthiasmedia.com.au/contact/overseas.htm** for details about recommended retailers in your part of the world.

2. Direct from us over the internet:
   – in the US: www.matthiasmedia.com
   – in Australia and the rest of the world: www.matthiasmedia.com.au

3. Direct from us by phone:
   – within Australia: 1800 814 360 (Sydney: 9663 1478)
   – international: +61 2 9663 1478

4. Trade enquiries worldwide:
   – email us: sales@matthiasmedia.com.au

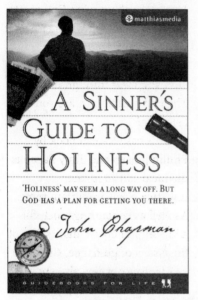

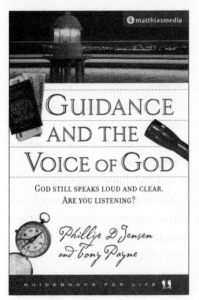

Also by Phillip Jensen and Tony Payne ...

Pure Sex

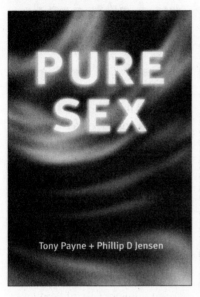

Tony Payne + Phillip D Jensen

Sex—pure, unadulterated and free. Stripped of all the guilt and restrictions of a bygone age. Liberated from the boring claustrophobia of marriage. At last, the freedom to express your own sexuality in whatever way you choose.

Such was the promise of the sexual revolution that swept the Western world in the 1960s and 70s. It didn't deliver. More than 30 years on, we find ourselves not in a sexual utopia, but in a sexual war zone, with broken relationships, hurt, guilt, and confusion on all sides.

Could it be that there is another way—one that actually makes sense of our sexuality, and allows us to express and enjoy it? Phillip Jensen and Tony Payne suggest that there is, and that it can be found in a most surprising place—in the ancient teachings of the Christian Bible.

Pure Sex is a book for all who are curious, confused, dissatisfied, hurt or struggling with sexuality, and who want some answers.

Also available as an audio book.

FOR MORE INFORMATION OR TO ORDER CONTACT:

Matthias Media
Telephone: +61 2 9663 1478 | Facsimile: +61 2 9663 3265
Email: sales@matthiasmedia.com.au

www.matthiasmedia.com.au

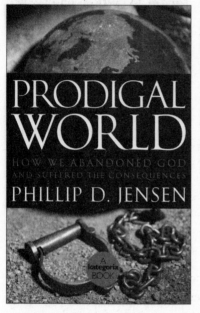